George Fox Bacon

Leading business Men of Marlboro, Hudson, So. Framingham, Natick, and Vicinity

Embracing also Saxonville and Cochituate

George Fox Bacon

Leading business Men of Marlboro, Hudson, So. Framingham, Natick, and Vicinity
Embracing also Saxonville and Cochituate

ISBN/EAN: 9783337081577

Printed in Europe, USA, Canada, Australia, Japan

Cover: Foto ©ninafisch / pixelio.de

More available books at **www.hansebooks.com**

MARLBORO, HUDSON,

SO. FRAMINGHAM, NATICK,

AND VICINITY;

EMBRACING ALSO

SAXONVILLE AND COCHITUATE.

ILLUSTRATED.

BOSTON:
MERCANTILE PUBLISHING COMPANY,
No. 258 Purchase Street.
1890.

PREFACE.

—

In this historical and statistical review of the commercial and manufacturing interests of this section, it has been our purpose in as thorough a manner as was possible to justly describe those enterprises which have contributed so largely during the last half century to the material advancement of these towns. History plainly shows that many large cities have owed their prosperity and growth chiefly to advantages of situation, great influx of foreign people, and similar causes. Of the towns in this section it is the genius and efforts of their people that have brought the present prosperity. This fact, that the history of these towns has practically been made almost entirely by her business men, lends particular significance to the close juxtaposition in which the account of her general and business interests are here placed.

MERCANTILE PUBLISHING CO.

[*For Contents see last pages.*]

HISTORICAL SKETCH

OF

MARLBORO.

Nearly 250 years have elapsed since the quaintly-worded petition was presented which resulted in the granting of the tract of land from which the present town of Marlborough was to be formed, and yet between the lines of that petition may be found unmistakable proof that human nature is much the same in all ages and among all peoples. The petitioners were thirteen prominent citizens of Sudbury and evidently believed in the adage "unto him that hath shall be given," for among the reasons they give why their prayer should be granted are the following :

"God hath been pleased to increase our children, which are now divers of them grown to man's estate, and wee, many of us, grown into years, so as wee should bee glad to see them settled before the Lord take us away from hence, as also God having given us some considerable cattle, so that we are so straightened that we cannot so comfortably subsist as could bee desired ; and some of us having taken some pains to view the country, we have found a place which lyeth westward, about eight miles from Sudbury, which wee conceive might bee comfortable for our subsistence."

They asked for a tract eight miles square but were given one about six miles square, containing 29,419 acres. This grant was made May 14, 1656, and September 25 of the same year the first meeting of the proprietors was held. Their plantation was called "Whipsufferage," this odd name being of Indian origin, or rather a corruption of the Indian "Whip-suppericke," the title of an adjacent hill. In November, 1660, there were set off and confirmed to their proprietors thirty-eight house-lots, among which were one for the minister and one for the smith ; the rest of the land being left subject to future grants and being known as "cow commons." The town was incorporated May 31, 1660, being named Marlborow in honor of the English town of the same name. It is supposed that this title was chosen because some of the early settlers came from that town but there is no certainty on this point, although it is evident that it could not, like the English Marlborow, be so called on account of the abundance of marl in the vicinity. Unfortunately the town records covering the first thirty-nine years in its history are missing, and consequently accurate infor-

mation of the proceedings of the townspeople during that period is very scarce,
what little is known being obtained from outside sources and in a fragmentary condition. The original Marlborough covered much more ground than the present
town as from it has been formed Westborough, Northborough, Southborough and
Hudson. At the time of incorporation the population was 55, at the end of the
first decade it had become 210 and remained at that point for another ten years,
when it began to increase steadily, so that in 1700 it had become 530. A half-
century later there were 1000 inhabitants, and in 1800 there were 1635, while during

MAIN ST. MARLBORO LOOKING WEST.

the next forty years some 500 more were added. The development of the town's
manufactures then began in earnest, and attracted so many to the community that
from 1850 to 1860 the population was almost doubled, increasing from 2941 to 5910.

Marlborough is bounded by Hudson and Berlin on the north, by Southborough
and Northborough on the south, on the west by Berlin and Northborough, and on
the east by Sudbury and Framingham. The entire township is situated on elevated
land, and to this fact, taken in conjunction with the purity of the air and the water,
may reasonably be ascribed the remarkable showing made by the townspeople as
regards health and longevity. The highest point is 650 feet above sea-level, and is
known as Mount Sligo, the name having formerly been spelled "Slygo," and having
been applied in derisive remembrance of one who lived there in Revolutionary times
and was supposed for a long while to have gone to the front as did about every able-
bodied man in the community. This particular individual, however, thought discretion the better part of valor, for instead of becoming a soldier, he hid in a cave connected by an underground passage with his house, only visiting the latter at night.
Hence the name, "Sly Go," to indicate the manner of his journeys between the cave

and the house. But the remainder of the townspeople were of quite a different disposition, and from the time when the first faint mutterings of discontent were heard down to the close of the struggle for independence they were not only outspoken in their advocacy of resistance but gave freely of their means and risked their lives to make such resistance effective. An example of the position they took from the first is afforded by the instructions given in September, 1774, to their representative, Peter Bent : " Pay no acknowledgment to any unconstitutional and new-fangled counsellors, and that you do not give your consent to any act or thing that may be

MAIN ST. MARLBORO, LOOKING EAST.

construed a tacit acknowledgment to any of the late oppressive, wicked and unjust acts of the British Parliament, for altering the government of the Province of Massachusetts Bay."

As it gradually became evident that the sword must finally be depended upon to cut the knots that statesmanship could not or would not untie, the people of Marlborough prepared themselves for the worst ; procured fifty-five additional guns with bayonets, added to their stores of ammunition, and went actively to work to organize and equip a force of militia. A company of minute-men was raised, drilled and assured bounty if called upon for active service, and in short, the curt advice : " In time of peace prepare for war," was followed to the extent of the people's means. How earnestly they devoted themselves to the cause is eloquently indicated by the fact that April 19, 1775, four companies, numbering 180 men, were put into the field at a moment's warning. The population of the town was then but 1300, making this a most impressive showing. The minute-men first sent out were absent but forty days and had no chance to attain distinction, but they were ready when called upon for whatever might ensue and many of them on their return home enlisted for longer or shorter periods, some of them enlisting for the full three years' term, while others enlisted "during the war." Take it all in all, Marlborough has abundant reason to be proud of her Revolutionary record; and the same may be said of her course during the late Rebellion, for her citizens, no matter what their political belief, were a unit in supporting the government and were prompt to make that fact known when news of the attack upon Fort Sumter was received. A town meeting was at once called at which the citizens tendered "our cordial and united support to the government of the United States; and pledge our lives and our fortunes for whatever service our country may require." The sum of ten thousand

TOWN HALL, MARLBORO.

dollars was afterward appropriated for war purposes, and a great deal more was subsequently expended in bounties and in many other ways, the total amount put out, exclusive of State aid being $51,584.11. Of the 869 men furnished by the town that actually engaged in the war, 574 served three years, 91 served one year, 108 served nine months and 96 served 100 days.

The first settlers of Marlborough fully appreciated the value of an education, but their means were very limited and it was only by a hard struggle that they were able to offer even the meagre facilities they did. For some years there was no regular school-house, but in December, 1698, it was voted to build one. More were built from time to time, and in 1771 Captain Ephraim Brigham left £111 for educational purposes; the interest of this sum being applied to the maintenance of what was known as the Brigham School, in which was supplemented the work of the town schools, the scholars being given an opportunity to perfect themselves in writing and arithmetic. A private academy was established in 1826 and was known as Gates Academy, after two years, owing to the gift of $2000 made by Silas and Abraham Gates, father and son. This institution was prosperous for a time, but it was finally merged into the high school in 1849. The school

THE "ELMS."

system of to-day is worthy of unstinted praise. It is but little more than half a century since the manufactures of Marlborough amounted to more than enough to supply local needs and a volume might be written on this topic alone for it is of the deepest interest, not only on account of the important bearing it has on the prosperity of the town, but also by reason of the manner in which our industries have been developed from very small beginnings. The production of boots and shoes is now carried on here on an immense scale, and present indications are that it is destined to be much more extensively developed in the future. Andrew Boyd was the first one to put into practice the making of boots

FIRST BAPTIST CHURCH.

and shoes by the "team" or "gang" system, this being introduced in 1836. It proved an immediate and permanent success and has since been improved upon until it has reached a very high stage of perfection. The sewing machine came into use in 1852, and there is now very little hand work, from the time the leather is cut to the sending out of the finished shoe. The productions of Marlborough are shipped to all parts of the Union and have a standard reputation which ensures a brisk and lasting demand for them. The mercantile establishments of the town are on a par with those devoted to manufacturing, being unsurpassed in their special lines.

LEADING BUSINESS MEN

OF

MARLBORO.

John F. Davey, Practical Machinist, Manufacturer of Davey's Pegging Machines, No. 15 Florence Street, Marlboro, Mass.—Mr. John F. Davey is a native of Canada, and has carried on operations in this town for more than a decade, having started here in 1878 as a member of the firm of Beven & Davey. In 1880 he became sole proprietor and remained so until 1882, when the firm of Davey & Exley was formed and continued the business up to 1884, since which date Mr. Davey has carried on operations alone. He is a practical machinist in the full sense of the term, for he has had long and varied experience in the doing of machine work in general, and in the making and repairing of shoe machinery in particular. He is the manufacturer of Davey's Pegging Machine, and gives special attention to the repairing of pegging and sewing machines of all kinds; a full assortment of duplicate parts of the New Era, Champion and Varney Pegging Machines being constantly carried. The shop is located at No. 15 Florence street, and is 30 × 60 feet in dimensions, being well equipped with improved tools and appliances which, with the aid of from four to six skilled assistants, enable the repairing of shoe machinery of all kinds to be successfully undertaken, the work being done at short notice and uniformly moderate charges being made.

THE DAVEY PATENT PEGGING MACHINE. Patented Nov. 5th 1889.

Geo. J. Hobbs, manufacturer of Cutting Dies, for Boots, Shoes, Paper Collars, Cuffs, Suspenders, etc., T. J. Beaudry, manager, Florence Street, Marlboro, Mass.—This firm was originally established by S. K. Taylor about thirty years ago, and after several changes, came into the possession of Hobbs & Mellen in 1875. Mr. Hobbs succeeding the above firm in 1879, with T. J. Beaudry as manager. After carrying on the business successfully for a period of ten years Mr. Hobbs became deceased. He was a native of Sturbridge, Mass., and was highly esteemed by all who knew him. The business is being continued by T. J. Beaudry, who has ably managed it since 1879. His shop is located on Florence street, and is fitted up with all necessary machinery, etc., to admit of the filling of all orders at short notice. Only first class workmen are employed and no pains is spared to keep up the reputation which this concern long ago established. His productions are used in many prominent New England factories, and his facilities for giving prompt attention to every order have much to do with the magnitude of his trade, for "time is money" in all branches of business, but particularly in that followed by the manufacturer, who therefore especially appreciates the advantages of having commissions executed without delay. The prices quoted are also entirely satisfactory, for, owing to the perfection of the equipment and the care taken to exercise economy in every detail of manufacture, he is in a position to sell as low as the lowest, that is to say, of course, the merits of the goods offered being equal. Employment is afforded to several competent assistants, and close personal attention is given to every department of the business.

CHARLES F. HOLYOKE,

INSURANCE AGENCY,

142 Main Street, - - Marlboro, Mass

ÆTNA,	Of Hartford.
CONNECTICUT,	Of Hartford.
FIREMAN'S FUND,	Of San Francisco.
GERMAN AMERICAN,	Of New York.
HANOVER,	Of New York.
HARTFORD,	Of Hartford.
HOME,	Of New York.
INSURANCE CO. OF NO. AMERICA,	Of Philadelphia.
LIVERPOOL AND LONDON AND GLOBE,	
MERCHANTS,	Of Newark.
NATIONAL,	Of Hartford.
NIAGARA,	Of New York.
ORIENT,	Of Hartford.
PHENIX,	Of Brooklyn.
QUEEN,	Of England.
SPRINGFIELD,	Of Springfield.

Frank & Duston, manufacturers of Paper Boxes of all kinds. Successors to the Marlboro Paper Box Co. (A. R. Frank, Arthur G. Duston,) Marlboro, Mass.—Considering the comparatively few years which paper boxes have been on the market, the present demand for them must be characterized as phenomenal, for so great is this demand that due appreciation of it is practically impossible, from the fact that the figures relating to it are too large to be comprehended by the mind. Paper boxes are used in almost all kinds of business, but they are particularly popular among those engaged in the shoe trade, and some idea of the number devoted to this purpose may be gained from the fact that a single concern in this town—that of Frank & Duston—operates a factory having a capacity to turn out 15,000 shoe boxes per day. This firm manufacture all kinds of paper boxes, but make a specialty of shoe boxes. This business was founded in 1885 by the Marlboro Paper Box Company, and passed under the control of the present proprietors in 1889. Mr. A. R. Frank was manager of the company for some years and is thoroughly familiar with the business in every detail. He is a native of Poland, Maine, and is associated with another Maine man, Mr. Arthur G. Duston, this gentleman having been born in Auburn. The firm utilize a four-story factory at the corner of High and Exchange streets, which is equipped with the latest improved machinery, driven by a 20-horse power engine. Employment is given to seventy assistants and the largest orders can be filled at short notice, while no firm is prepared to quote lower prices on equally desirable goods.

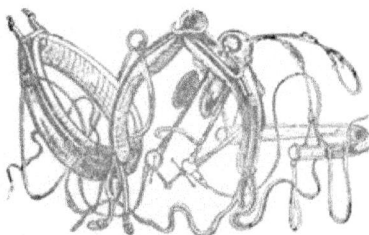

Edward L. Tucker, manufacturer of and dealer in Harness, Trunks, Whips, Bags, Robes, etc., etc. Repairing, Oiling and Cleaning promptly attended to. 84 Main Street, Marlboro, Mass.—It is difficult to properly estimate the amount of strain which any harness may be called upon to bear, for a fairly stout horse can for a moment or two pull with several times the force he exercises under ordinary circumstances, and when a pair of willing animals trained to work together, throw their whole weight on the harness in trying to start a heavy load on a hill or elsewhere, it puts leather and workmanship to a severe test, especially if the harness be not a new one. Accidents from the breakage of harness, etc., are too common not to excite remark, and experienced drivers take good care to procure everything in this line from sources they can depend upon. Some excellent harness is made and sold in Marlboro, and it would be both foolish and untrue to say that any one manufacturer had a monopoly of producing dependable goods, but it is generally conceded that those made and sold by Mr. Edward L. Tucker at No. 84 Main street, Marlboro, are thoroughly reliable and will bear the severest examination and comparison. This enterprise was started in 1878 by Cheney & Coulter who were succeeded in 1881 by Mr. D. Coulter, and he in 1887 by the present proprietor. Mr. Tucker is a native of Skowhegan, Maine, and has given a good deal of attention to the business. He manufactures and deals at retail in harnesses of all kinds, also trunks, bags, whips, robes, etc., etc., all work being promptly executed and the prices quoted on both goods and work being as low as is consistent with the quality thereof.

Albert E. Rowles, successor to George H. Adams, dealer in Provisions and Groceries, Teas and Coffees, Spices, Canned Fruits, Pickles, etc., Winthrop Street, near Lincoln, Marlboro, Mass. —One of the best known and popular establishments in Marlboro is that conducted by Mr. Albert E. Rowles, on Winthrop street, near Lincoln, and we believe that there is not another in the entire town that can excel it in its special line. It was established originally by Mr. Geo. H. Adams, who was succeeded by Messrs. Rowles & Whitman in 1885, and in 1887 Mr. Rowles assumed the entire control of the business. The stock carried is made up of provisions, meat and groceries of all kinds, a specialty being made of teas and coffees, spices, canned fruits, pickles, etc. The premises occupied are of the dimensions of 30×40 feet, and the stock carried is a most varied and extensive one. The show windows are full of choice food supplies of all kinds, and in fact everything in the line of provisions and groceries are to be found here at the proper seasons, and are offered at prices considerably below those quoted at stores that make much greater pretensions, but actually supply no better articles. The entire stock handled is conceded to be of superior quality, and the extensive retail business done is of itself enough to show the estimation in which the goods are held. The very lowest market rates are always obtainable here, and the employment of efficient assistants guarantees that prompt and polite attention will be given to every customer. This is a representative store and fully deserves its popularity. Mr. Rowles is a native of England, and is well known and highly esteemed in Marlboro as an enterprising and reliable business man.

W. P. Dorr, Practical Wood Turner, Florence Street, Marlboro, Mass.—Wood-working is extensively carried on in Marlboro and vicinity, and there are many excellently equipped establishments devoted to this line of industry but not one of them has a higher reputation in its own special line than that conducted by Mr. W. P. Dorr, on Florence street. Mr. Dorr is a native of Bucksport, Maine, and is a practical wood-turner of wide and varied experience. His shop is fitted up with improved machinery and every facility is at hand to admit of scroll and jig sawing of all kinds being done at very short notice and in a uniformly satisfactory manner. Brackets of all kinds are made to order at moderate rates, and large and small commissions are given equally careful attention. Mr. Dorr makes a specialty of the designing and turning of piazza columns, and has originated many tasteful and attractive styles. Those who contemplate building and who wish their houses to have some individuality, should communicate with Mr. Dorr, for it is only by careful attention to details that individuality is to be attained, and no details are more prominent than are piazza columns, so that taste and skill shown in their designing will do much to heighten the effect conveyed by the entire house.

Anselme Sansoucy, Cigar Manufacturer and Importer, Marlboro, Mass.—There is no question but that there is more of a demand for high-grade cigars than was formerly the case, and retailers who appreciate this fact and act accordingly, are the ones who stand the best chance of building up and retaining a desirable class of trade. Of course, there are some grades so high in price that none but the rich can afford them, but we do not refer to these, but rather to brands that can be retailed at a reasonable figure and still are far superior to the average cheap cigar. Mr. Anselme Sansoucy makes a specialty of such goods, and is prepared to supply them at wholesale in any desired quantity at short notice. He manufactures and imports many different grades, and quotes the lowest market rates on every order. Mr. Sansoucy was born in Canada, and began business in Marlboro in 1886. He has gained a high reputation among the trade for straightforward and enterprising business methods and his patronage is consequently steadily and rapidly increasing. Employment is given to five efficient assistants, and orders by mail are assured immediate and painstaking attention.

E. P. Howe, Machinist and Shoe Tool Manufacturer. Small Machinery of all kinds a Specialty, Marlboro.—Mr. E. P. Howe is a native of Marlboro, and has been in business here altogether about two years, having previously been located in Northboro. He is a machinist and shoe tool manufacturer, and has had about seventeen years' experience in that line of work, having carried on operations in Northboro for about fifteen years. His present shop is located on Florence street, and is fitted up with the most improved tools and other facilities, enabling all orders to be filled at short notice and in first-class style. Particular attention is given to the making of shoe tools to order, and the results attained are sure to prove entirely satisfactory to the most critical. Machinery repairing of all kinds is given prompt and painstaking attention, the work being done in a neat and durable manner and no fancy charges being made. Practical experience is the only thing that will fit a man to successfully undertake the carrying out of orders of this kind, and the reputation Mr. Howe has won is the natural result of his long and varied training and his efforts to fully satisfy every reasonable customer. A specialty is made of small machinery of all kinds, and low prices are quoted in every department of the business.

Boynton & Co. (successors to J. G. Stetson & Co.), dealers in Dry and Fancy Goods, Ladies' and Gents' Furnishings, Worsteds, Trimmings and Small Wares, 168 and 170 Fairmount Block, Marlboro, Mass.—It is doubtless perfectly fair to say that there is not a concern in town more favorably known to the fair sex than that of Messrs. Boynton & Co., for this firm deal in goods that are of special interest to the ladies, and quote prices that make their store a favorite resort with the most discriminating buyers. The business was founded a number of years ago by Messrs. Wilson & Howe, who were succeeded by Messrs. Howe & Stetson; this firm giving place to Messrs. J. G. Stetson & Co., and the present proprietors assuming control in 1886. Messrs. J. Farley Boynton, and George F. Boynton are both natives of Brookline, Mass., and the firm have another establishment in that beautiful town, this being under the direct management of the junior partner, while Mr. J. Farley Boynton has control of the Marlboro store. The premises utilized in this town, have an area of 2000 square feet, and are located at Nos. 168 and 170 Fairmount Block. They contain a very heavy and varied stock of foreign and domestic dry and fancy goods, ladies' and gents' furnishings worsteds, trimmings and small wares, and the assortment is so complete that it is safe to say all tastes and purses can be suited. Employment is given to seven efficient and polite assistants, and customers are assured immediate and careful attention, while it may not be out of place to state that every article—cheap or costly—is sold strictly on its merits and is guaranteed to prove precisely as represented in every respect.

Miss Mary Maguire, Millinery. 45 Mechanic Street, opposite the Bank, Marlboro, Mass.—Ladies are very apt to scorn the advice of a mere man (and perhaps not without reason), concerning matters of dress and personal adornment, and therefore we will not be so rash as to ask them on our recommendation to patronize the establishment conducted by Miss Mary Maguire, located at No. 45 Mechanic street, but we may be permitted to say that many of the best-known ladies of Marlboro and vicinity speak in the highest terms of the facilities afforded at the store in question, and indeed it seems as though no person of taste could inspect what Miss Maguire has to offer without becoming convinced of her fitness for the management of such an enterprise. Operations were commenced in 1875 by Mrs. G. W. Holt, she being succeeded by Miss Maguire in 1889. The premises measure 24×36 feet and contain a fine selection of millinery and millinery goods, and the most fastidious purchaser can scarcely fail to find something perfectly suited to her wants. Miss Maguire is always ready to give such advice as her taste and extended experience may suggest should such aid be desired. She is a native of Marlboro and has gained many friends and patrons throughout this community, as the work done at her establishment is not only beautiful but durable as well, and the prices are remarkably low, when the quality of the service rendered is considered.

People's National Bank, 121 Main Street, Marlboro, Mass.—First class banking facilities cannot help making a manufacturing community more prosperous than would otherwise be possible, and every year makes such facilities more absolutely indispensable to any community that would attain a prominent and leading position. It is difficult to understand how those who affect to believe that a national bank can be of no pronounced service in the advancement of manufacturing and mercantile interests, can reconcile that belief with the logic of facts for abundant instances can be pointed out where the establishment of such an institution has greatly stimulated local enterprises and has been the source of pronounced and permanent prosperity. Nor is it necessary to go far away from home to find a case in point, as no more typical one could be wished than that afforded by the success which has attended the operations of the People's National Bank, since the incorporation of that institution in 1878. The name of this bank is an unusually appropriate one in view of the methods which have thus far characterized the management of the undertaking, for we think all well informed and unprejudiced readers will agree that the institution has been and is run in the interests of the whole people, and not for the advancement of the fortunes of any clique. Indeed, the names of those who have the bank in charge would of themselves go far to make this seem the only course which could reasonably be predicted, for the People's National Bank is in the hands of representative citizens who have shown in many ways that they have the best interests of the entire community at heart. The bank has a capital of $100,000 and its financial condition is beyond criticism. Drafts issued by this institution are payable in parts of America and Great Britain, and collections will be made in all parts of the United States, all commissions being carefully and promptly executed. The premises occupied are located in Temple Block, No. 121 Main street, and are conveniently fitted up, so that the extensive business done is trans-

acted with very little delay—a point which is appreciated by those to whom "time is money." The following is a list of officers and directors:

President, D. W. Hitchcock.
Vice-president, John O'Connell.
Cashier, John L. Stone.
Directors, D. W. Hitchcock, John O'Connell, John L. Stone, S. N. Aldrich, L. S. Brigham, A. C. Weeks, B. F. Greeley, S. H. Howe, W. M. Warren, Abel Howe, C. B. Greenwood, L. P. Howe, Emerson Stone.

Brigham & Eager, dealers in Watches, Clocks and Jewelry, Marlboro, Mass.—An establishment which residents of this vicinity have learned to patronize whenever possible is that conducted by Messrs. Brigham & Eager, and the reasons for this preference are not hard to give after an inspection of the goods offered, and a comparison of the prices asked, with those in force at other stores. The inception of this undertaking was in 1857, under the name of L. S. Brigham, and so continued until 1883, when the present partnership was formed, and the firm name became as at present, Brigham & Eager. The experience gained and the favorable relations established by the proprietors since that time have put them in a position to meet all competition, and to guarantee that their inducements are unsurpassed and in most cases unequalled elsewhere. Mr. L. S. Brigham is a native of Francistown, N. H., and Mr. H. W. Eager of Northboro, Mass., and are too well known and highly esteemed in this vicinity to require extended personal mention. The premises utilized are of the dimensions of 22×35 feet, and are fully stocked with an extremely varied assortment of watches, clocks and jewelry of all descriptions. Also pianos are dealt in, and competent assistants are at hand to extend polite and prompt attention to every customer. Those in need of a watch that will be something more than an ornament should give this establishment a call, for the productions of all the leading makers are kept in stock and can be furnished at a very fair price, that will give perfect satisfaction in every respect. All goods are warranted to prove as represented and sold at bottom prices.

H. R. W. Este, dealer in Milk, Butter, Skimmilk and Cream, 2 Main Street and 1 Maple Street, Marlboro, Mass.—The question of where pure, fresh milk can be obtained at a reasonable price is one of the first importance to every family, for inferior milk is neither palatable nor healthful, and it is far better to go without altogether than use that which is not first class. Happily there is no need of the residents of Marlboro and vicinity having to do without "nature's food," for one of the most extensive dealers in milk in this section carries on operations here at No. 2 Main street and No. 1 Maple street, and is prepared to supply milk and cream of standard quality in quantities to suit, doing both a wholesale and retail business and quoting the lowest market rates at all times. We refer to Mr. H. R. W. Este, who is a native of Southboro, and began business here in 1886. Mr. Este also deals largely in butter, and offers grades that cannot fail to suit even the most fastidious. He employs three assistants, and customers are sure of receiving prompt and polite attention.

Noah Willard, Boarding, Sale, Feed, Hack and Livery Stable, 68 Main Street, Marlboro, Mass.—Mr. Noah Willard has had considerable experience in the livery business, for he has been engaged in this line of industry here in Marlboro since 1878 having succeeded Mr. Joseph Rock at that date, and since 1881 has been located at No. 68 Main street. His familiarity with what the public want in the line of livery service enables him to cater very successfully to all wishing to hire a team for business or pleasure purposes, and the pleasant associations which so many visitors to Marlboro have in connection with their stay here, are largely due in a number of cases to the excellent facilities afforded them by Mr. Willard to view the town and its surroundings. His teams are first class in every respect, the horses being speedy and willing roadsters, while the vehicles are modern in style and easy and comfortable to ride in. Orders can be filled at very short notice and at rates which are very reasonable considering the superior accommodations provided. The premises utilized are as follows: the carriage room (lower floor) is 49 × 75 feet in size, the upper floor being 40 × 50 feet, while the middle or second floor which is used for hay and grain is 40×75 feet. The new stable which is three stories, contains forty stalls, and every facility is at hand for the maintenance not only of a first class livery service, but also for the carrying on of the boarding, sale and feed business. Barges for picnics and parties will be supplied at moderate rates. Mr. Willard is a native of Richford, Vt., and is very generally known throughout this section of Massachusetts. He deals in baled hay and straw, also attends to horse clipping which is neatly done, and is also the manufacturer of the "Favorite Condition Powders," liniments, etc., for horses, cattle, sheep and hogs, etc. We take pleasure in making favorable mention of Mr. Willard's establishment, for it is unquestionably of benefit to the community and is carried on in a liberal manner that is deserving of unreserved commendation. Mr. Willard, in addition to the above business also deals extensively in grain. Sales amounting to about 250 bushels a week.

E. J. Elliott, Contractor and Builder ; care and sale of Real Estate a Specialty, and also a dealer in Real Estate. Residence 99 Lincoln Street, Marlboro, Mass.— Mr. E. J. Elliott is a native of Boscarven, N. H., and has carried on operations in Marlboro since 1882. He has come to be regarded as an authority on local real estate, for he makes the care and sale of such property a specialty, and is thoroughly well informed concerning it. Those wishing to buy or sell anything in this line would do well to give Mr. Elliott a call and thereby save themselves time and trouble, while non-resident owners or others who are not in a position to give their real estate the attention it requires, will find him prepared to assume the care of the same at a moderate charge, and may safely depend upon having their interests carefully and intelligently protected. Mr. Elliott is also a contractor and builder. He is prepared to furnish estimates at short notice on any kind of wooden buildings. Any one in want of a house will do well to call on Mr. Elliott as he sells them on easy terms of payment and at moderate prices. His residence is at No. 99 Lincoln street.

W. C. Blake & Co , Clothing, Gents' Furnishings, Hats and Caps, Trunks, Bags and Umbrellas, 164 Main Street, Marlboro.—The purchasing public are more interested in the fact of a thing being so, than in the reasons why it is so; or in other words, are content to remain in ignorance of how a certain dealer can offer special inducements as long as they are satisfied that the inducements are genuine. Still, it is always worth while to inquire into the reason of things, and some of the many who appreciate the various bargains offered by Messrs. W. C. Blake & Co., in the line of clothing, etc., may be curious to know "how the thing is done." Well, there are many factors to be considered if the matter is to be thoroughly understood, but briefly stated, the explanation is simply this: Long experience, careful buying, enterprising methods, and very extensive trade. Mr. Blake maintains similar establishments at Providence, R. I., Middletown, Conn., also one in Meriden, Conn., and, as may well be imagined, disposes of an immense quantity of clothing in the course of a year. He is a native of Milford, Mass., and began operations in Marlboro in 1876, having Mr. W. H. Gile for a partner until 1881, since which date Mr. Blake has been sole proprietor, no change, however, being made in the firm name. The premises utilized are located at No 164 Main street, and are of the dimensions of 23 × 80 feet. A very large and desirable stock of clothing, gentlemen's furnishings, hats and caps, trunks, bags, canes and umbrellas and other articles is constantly carried, and the very latest fashionable novelties are fully represented in it. As for the prices quoted, they are in every instance as low as the lowest, quality considered, and the buyer knows that he is getting just what he pays for, every time. Employment is given to six efficient assistants, and callers are waited upon promptly, politely and carefully.

Orient Tea Company, E. F. Pond, Proprietor, 157 Main Street, Marlboro, Mass.—There is an old story to the effect that a college professor, after exhaustive calculations, decided that his body was lighter than water and consequently should float, and to prove his theory correct he jumped overboard in deep water, and, being no swimmer, was drowned, as despite his theory his body was obstinate enough to sink. We are reminded of this story by the course of those who, having formed a theory that a tea store cannot give presents to customers and sell superior goods at bottom prices, refuse to patronize such establishments and are satisfied to buy teas and coffees elsewhere, the result being inferior goods and no presents at all. Theory is all very well but practice tells the story, and it is only necessary to deal awhile at the Orient Tea Store, No. 157 Main street, in order to establish the facts that the quality of the goods there sold is unsurpassed, the prices are low as the lowest, and beautiful and useful presents, consisting of tea sets, dinner sets, etc., are given to every purchaser of teas and coffees. The present proprietor of this popular establishment, Mr. E. F. Pond, is a native of Foxboro, Mass., and assumed possession in 1886. He carries a very large stock at all times, employs two assistants, and spares no pains to ensure prompt and courteous attention and entire satisfaction to every customer.

C. S. Thompson, Bookseller and Stationer, dealer in Newspapers, Periodicals and Fancy Goods, 109 Main Street, Lawrence Block, Marlboro, Mass.—The establishment conducted by Mr. C. S. Thompson, at No. 109 Main street, Lawrence Block, is deservedly popular with the purchasing public, for the stock it contains is always complete and attractive and the prices quoted are in accordance with the lowest market rates. The premises measure 28×42 feet and the assortment offered comprises books, stationery, newspapers, periodicals and fancy goods. Mr. Thompson is a native of Holliston, Mass., and succeeded Mr. Barker in April, 1889. He is agent for the Boston daily papers and is prepared to receive subscriptions for all the leading periodicals at publishers' rates. The latest popular novels, etc, are placed on sale immediately after publication, and books not in stock will be obtained at short notice without extra charge. The latest novelties in stationery are to be had here at bottom prices, as well as gold pens and pencils of the best quality, and writing materials in general. Prompt and courteous attention is assured to every customer, goods being cheerfully shown and no trouble being spared to ensure complete satisfaction to all. Mr. Thompson's specialty is blank books, ready made and to order. his increasing business in this line abundantly testifies to his well-earned reputation.

Henry K. W. Andrews, Contractor and Builder of all kinds of Wooden and Brick Buildings. Shop, Florence Street, over Box Shop. Residence, Elm Street, Marlboro, Mass.—It is not an infrequent thing to hear those who have built their own houses warn their friends not to do so themselves, but rather to buy a house "ready-made," and thus avoid the annoyances and anxieties incidental to building. When such warning is given, it is almost invariably the result of dealing with incompetent or irresponsible builders, for those who have had their houses erected by men who know their business and make a practice of carrying out their agreements, are given no reason to regret the course they have taken. A little care taken in the placing of orders to begin with will save much subsequent trouble, and it should not be difficult to place orders for building satisfactorily in this vicinity, for there are various entirely competent and reliable contractors and builders here located, prominent among which is Mr. Henry K. W. Andrews, whose shop is on Florence street, over the box shop. Mr. Andrews was born in Marlboro, served in the army during the Rebellion, and has been in his present business for more than a score of years, during which time he has built up a very high reputation for prompt attention to orders and the doing of first-class work. He is prepared to undertake the erection of all kinds of wooden and brick buildings, and to figure very closely on all plans submitted. Employment is given to from thirty-five to fifty assistants and ALL orders are assured prompt and careful attention. Mr. Andrews guarantees first-class work and gives close personal supervision to his business, sparing no pains to maintain the enviable reputation so long enjoyed. This firm are quite extensive contractors for factories and other large buildings, having built many of this character in the past few years.

Ellis Manufacturing Company, Sole Proprietors Acme Filter, 2 Fairmount Street, Marlboro, Mass.—No arguments are required to show the advantages of using pure water, and as practically no water drawn from pipes will even approach purity unless it be filtered, it follows that a filter of some sort is a necessity in every family using such water. To be adapted to popular use a filter must be simple and strong in construction, efficient in design, and low in price, and the Acme Filter so thoroughly "fills the bill," in every respect that its unrivalled popularity with all classes is not to be wondered at in the least. This filter is endorsed by well-known parties in every section where it has been introduced, and only needs a fair trial to demonstrate its superiority beyond the shadow of a doubt. It is manufactured by the Ellis Manufacturing Company, who carry on operations at No. 166 Main street, and No. 2 Fairmount street, Marlboro, Mass. The proprietors have unreserved confidence in the "Acme," and invite comparison with any competitor, claiming superiority in simplicity, durability and perfect execution. Every filter is warranted to be free from imperfections, and the proprietors agree to make good, any time within a year, any defect not caused by use, misuse or accident. In fact, the Acme is made for SERVICE, and not merely to sell, and this is just where it differs from two-thirds of the filters with which the market is flooded. The company will promptly send an illustrated circular giving full information on application, and will send sample filter to any address upon receipt of price, $1.50. A bib, to attach the filter to plain faucet, will be sent for 35 cents extra. Pure water is certainly worth some little trouble to get, and when it is assured at a merely nominal expense, it is difficult to see how anyone can be satisfied to go without it.

E. P. Richardson, Photographer, 193 Main Street, Marlboro, Mass.—Since the time that the great French artist discovered the art of daguerreotyping, photography has been making rapid and continual advances until to-day it occupies a position of commanding influence. The photographic studio now conducted by Mr. E. P. Richardson, at No. 193 Main street, was established in 1868 by his father, Mr. J. C. Richardson, who continued the business until his death, which occurred in 1882, and the popularity and success which has attended Mr. E. P. Richardson's subsequent progress, speak most conclusively for his skill as an artist, and the good taste of the people of Marlboro. Mr. Richardson occupies a fine studio at the above address, where he is prepared to offer his patrons the most satisfactory work in all branches of fine photography. Old pictures are copied and enlarged and all kinds of crayon work done at all prices, ranging from $5.00 to $50.00, in the most approved styles, also all size portraits finished in oil colors. Special attention is given to bromides in which he has attained unexcelled success. An examination of his work, and the testimony of his large circle of patrons will confirm all he claims for his talents and workmanship. Mr. Richardson is a native of Ashburnham, Mass. He served four years in the army during our late Civil war, and has made many friends in our midst by his courtesy and skill as an artist.

Levi Taylor, dealer in Carriages, Sleighs and Harnesses, a full line of Robes constantly on hand. Horse Shoeing. Jobbing and Carriage Repairing done promptly at reasonable prices, Mechanic Square, Marlboro.—Mr. Levi Taylor has had an experience of more than thirty years in his present line of business, and this being the case, it is not necessary to bring forward proofs that he is thoroughly acquainted with it in every detail. He is a native of Stowe, Mass., and served three years in the army, establishing himself in Marlboro in 1869. The premises occupied are located in Mechanic square, and comprise a two story building, measuring 25×50 feet, and a one-story ell, of the dimensions of 25×40 feet. They are fitted up with all necessary facilities for the carrying on of a general jobbing, horse-shoeing and carriage repairing business, and the employment of two competent assistants enables all orders to be filled at short notice. Mr. Taylor has for more than a score of years done his best to satisfy his customers, and may safely depend on the reputation he has won to assure him continued and generous patronage. Strength, neatness and durability are the characteristics of the work turned out here, and the prices are as low as can be named in connection with the attainment of the best possible results. Mr. Taylor deals in carriages, sleighs and harnesses, and carries a full line of robes at all times. Every article is sold under a guarantee that it will prove as represented, and the prices quoted will bear the strictest examination and comparison.

R. O. Clark, D. D. S., Surgeon Dentist, 156 Main Street, Marlboro, Mass.—It will undoubtedly be some years before the old characterization of the United States as "a nation of dyspeptics" will cease to have any foundation in fact, for the customs of a people are not to be revolutionized in a day, and the effects of those customs are sure to be noticeable for some time after the causes are removed, but it is unquestionably a fact that Americans live more healthfully to-day than ever before; being more careful of their diet, and paying more attention to the laws of hygiene in every way. Whether badly-chosen and improperly cooked food is responsible for the generally defective teeth of residents of this country or not, is an open question, but it is generally agreed that the connection between dyspepsia and defective teeth is much more close than was once thought possible. Even badly cooked food is robbed of much of its ill effects by thorough mastication, but proper mastication with defective teeth is practically impossible, and right here we have the explanation of the stubbornness with which indigestion resists medical treatment, for most continued dyspeptics have very poor teeth; poor teeth result in poor preparation of the food, and, the cause being continued, the effect is likewise continuous. The remedy is simple and obvious. Visit a competent dentist, have the teeth put in effective condition, use them and treat them as they should be used and treated, and the results attained cannot fail to be gratifying and permanent. There are so many excellent dentists practising in this vicinity that there need be no trouble in securing expert advice and treatment, and among them there is not one having a higher and more fully deserved reputation for skillful, gentle and thorough work than R. O. Clark, D. D. S., whose rooms are at No. 156 Main street. Dr. Clark is a native of North Weymouth, Mass., and is a graduate of the Boston Dental College. He has practiced his profession in Marlboro since 1881, having at that time succeeded S. J. Shaw, who had been located in this town for a quarter of a century. Dr. Clark has the latest improved tools, appliances and other facilities at his command, and is excellently well prepared to carry on dentistry in accordance with the most approved methods. His charges are uniformly moderate, and his work is fully warranted to give the best of satisfaction.

Henry Gates, wholesale and retail dealer in all kinds of Ladders, Step Ladders, Trestles, Window Jacks, Revolving Clothes Dryers, Clothes Horses, Boys' Clipper Sleds, Snow Shovels, Carriage Jacks, Adjustable Ladder Hooks, Lawn Settees, and Basket and Reed Chairs, No. 47 Main Street, Marlboro, Mass.—A ladder is one of the most simple and at the same time one of the most useful of contrivances, and as good material as well as good workmanship must enter into the construction of a ladder that shall combine lightness and strength in the proper degree, it is well to place orders with a thoroughly reputable dealer, and no one more deserving of such description can be mentioned than Mr. Henry Gates, doing business at No. 47 Main street. Another advantage in dealing with this gentleman lies in the fact that he is prepared to quote bottom prices, for he does an extensive wholesale and retail business, and enjoys the most favorable relations with manufacturers. Mr. Gates was born in Nova Scotia, and had eight years' experience in his present line of business in Providence before beginning operations here in 1886. He does not confine himself to handling ladders and step ladders by any means, but also deals largely in trestles, window jacks, revolving clothes dryers, clothes horses, boys' clipper sleds, snow shovels, carriage jacks, adjustable ladder hooks, lawn settees, basket and reed chairs, etc. A large stock is carried, and callers are assured prompt and polite attention, while the lowest market rates are quoted on all the articles handled. Mr. Gates has also recently taken the agency for Suffolk, Middlesex and Plymouth counties for the Combination Steam Cooker and Baking Pan, which is acknowledged to be the best steam cooker and baking pan that has ever been placed on the market.

C. F. Weeks, manufacturer of Fine Carriages and Wagons of every description, also Harnesses. Corner of Main and Lincoln Streets, Middlesex Square, Marlboro, Mass.—An establishment of special interest to horse owners is that carried on by Mr. C. F. Weeks, at the corner of Main and Lincoln streets, for Mr. Weeks is a manufacturer of fine carriages and wagons of every description, and is also extensively engaged in the manufacture and sale of superior harnesses of all kinds for both light and heavy work. He is a native of Rockville, Conn., and has been identified with his present enterprise since 1888, at that time succeeding Mr. O. P. Walker, who had carried it on for over twelve years. The premises have an area of 2400 square feet and are fitted up with the most improved machinery, etc., employment being given to five efficient and careful assistants, so that orders can be filled in an entirely satisfactory manner at short notice. Mr. Weeks is not one of those who try to "make a silk purse out of a sow's ear," and therefore when he receives a commission to make a first-class vehicle, he takes pains to select the very best stock obtainable. Such material, put together by skilled workmen, is sure to prove strong and durable, and consequently it is perfectly natural that the carriages and wagons made here should have an unsurpassed reputation for durability as well as for beauty and convenience of design. Horse shoeing and jobbing are given particular and painstaking attention, and moderate charges are made in this as in every other department of the business.

Warner's Music and Toy Store, J. H. Warner, Proprietor, Pianos and Organs, Sheet Music and Music Books, Picture Frames to order, 163 Main Street, Marlboro.—An establishment which is familiar to the many music-lovers of Marlboro and vicinity is that so successfully conducted by Mr. J. H. Warner at Nos. 159 and 163 Main street. This gentleman began business here in 1884, and during the period since elapsed has built up a trade of imposing proportions. He carries a fine assortment of sheet music and music books of every description, and his stock of pianos and organs is the largest in Middlesex County, and comprises both new and second-hand instruments, some really fine bargains being obtainable in this department. A hint of Mr. Warner's business enterprise and sagacity may be gained from the fact of his including in his line of business in addition to musical merchandise of every description, toys and fancy goods in large variety, and also the manufacture of picture frames to order at low prices, a large lot of new mouldings and samples always being carried in stock. Piano and organ tuning is made a specialty, and satisfaction is guaranteed. Violin bows are carefully repaired, and strings warranted first-class. The premises utilized cover an area of 2700 square feet and the business done is exclusively retail in character, requiring the services of competent and well-informed assistants. Mr. Warner is a native of Foxboro, Mass., and deals only in the productions of the most reliable manufacturers, and an instrument, warranted by him, may be purchased in the full assurance that it will prove to be precisely as represented.

J. L. Marshall, dealer in Meats and Provisions, 167 Lincoln Street, Marlboro, Mass.—There are business houses in every community that are so universally accorded a leading position as to place the matter beyond question, but in noticing the undisputed prominence of such enterprises, one is very apt to lose sight of the hard work and perseverance which placed them where they are. Take for instance the undertaking carried on by Mr. J. L. Marshall, at No. 167 Lincoln street, Marlboro, and what do we find? Its high position is not open to doubt, the large retail business is apparent to all, but still these things are not the creation of a day, a week or a year, but on the contrary are simply the legitimate out-come of industry, economy, ability and strong determination to excel. Whatever celebrity or public appreciation Mr. Marshall has attained has been fairly won, honestly bestowed, and if every young man could be made to see that to accomplish similar results in his own case he must make similar exertions, one fruitful cause of discontent in our modern society would be removed. To achieve it is necessary to earn it, and he who obtains it otherwise does so by fraud and need not expect it to be permanent. Mr. Marshall is a native of England, and succeeded to his present enterprise in 1885. His establishment covers an area of 20 × 50 feet, and all the available space is occupied by the heavy and varied stock on hand which includes meats and provisions of all kinds, as well as butter, cheese, eggs, beans, pork, canned goods, fruit, etc. These goods are offered at such prices as to ensure their prompt and certain sale, and the assortment is consequently being continuously renewed so that articles supplied are fresh and desirable in every way.

Miss R. L. Shumway, Millinery, Materials for Embroidery and Hair Goods, 161 Main Street, Marlboro, Mass.—It only requires a visit to the establishment of the lady whose card we print above to convince any one competent to judge, that it is managed with exceptional taste and skill, and the record this enterprise has made since it was inaugurated in 1882, is another proof that the public may confidently expect the best of service at this popular store. It is 15×50 feet in dimensions, and being centrally located at No. 161 Main street, it is as convenient of access as it is desirable to visit. Millinery, embroidery materials and hair goods are the commodities dealt in, and the very latest fashionable novelties in these lines are received at this establishment as soon as they are placed on the market. Trimmed and untrimmed hats and bonnets are furnished at reasonable prices together with ribbons, silks, feathers and other trimmings in great variety. A fine line of embroidery materials of all kinds is carried in stock, also a choice line of human hair goods, and it is but the simple truth to say that no other establishment in this town is better prepared to guarantee perfect satisfaction to the most fastidious customers. Miss Shumway's taste is too well known to require extended mention in these pages, and we will only add that she spares no pains to completely satisfy every patron.

Windsor House, Louis Houde, proprietor, 224 Main Street, Marlboro, Mass.—The services rendered to a community by the establishment and maintenance of a really first-class hotel are greatly underestimated in the majority of cases. No one who has given the subject any attention will deny that a liberally and intelligently managed public house will attract visitors to the city or town in which it is located. The fact is notorious, how the class of people who patronize a first-class hotel as a rule have money to spend and do spend it freely, and there is not a merchant in town but what is benefitted more or less directly by the presence of such visitors. It should therefore be a cause for congratulation among Marlboro business men that the Windsor House should be under its present management, for there is no denying that this is a first-class hotel, run in a first-class manner, and the effect of the liberal methods practiced by its proprietor is plainly to be seen in the character and extent of the patronage received. The Windsor House occupies a handsome and commodious building, erected in 1882 and first opened for hotel purposes by Mr. Louis Houde, the year following. In June, 1888, Mr. Houde was succeeded by Mr. Harry S. Phillips, but in December of the same year, Mr. Houde again became proprietor. He is a native of Canada, and is extremely popular with his guests, whom he spares no pains to serve in the most satisfactory manner. The hotel can accommodate seventy-five, and even when well filled the service is exceptionally prompt and obliging, employment being given to twelve assistants and uniform courtesy being insisted upon to every guest. The terms are moderate, and the sleeping accommodations, table, etc., will be found entirely satisfactory by the most fastidious.

Dacey & Son, Sale, Feed, Hack and Livery Stable; Horse Clipping by Rotary Power, Cor. Main Street and Ames Place, Marlboro, Mass.—There is a right way and a wrong way to do everything, and a man may have the right to choose the wrong way if he prefers but he certainly has no excuse for complaining of the results attained should he do so. Take it for instance in buying a horse. Purchasers can choose between buying of some travelling dealer or other whom nobody really knows, and dealing with an established local concern which has a reputation to maintain, and if they do business with the former and get badly "taken in," they really have but little reason to grumble, for it was only what might have been expected. Messrs. Dacey & Son have an enviable reputation for representing things as they are when dealing in horseflesh, and that such a policy pays best in the end is shown by their steadily increasing business in this line alone. They also carry on a feed, hack and livery stable, and do horse clipping by rotary power, being prepared to fill all orders at short notice. This enterprise was started by Messrs. Dacey & Cutting, in 1882, and passed under the control of the present firm in 1888; the partners being P. F. and T. M. Dacey. The stable contains twenty-two stalls and is located on the corner of Main street and Ames place. Employment is given to two competent assistants and callers can depend upon receiving polite attention.

T. A. Coolidge, manufacturer of Men's and Boys' Shoes, both light and heavy, 25 Howland Street, Marlboro, Mass.—The enterprise carried on by Mr. T. A. Coolidge is so truly representative, and has held a leading position among the most important undertakings located in Marlboro for so long a period of time, that not to give it especially prominent mention in a review of the industries of this section would be a most strange omission, and yet it is practically impossible to state anything new concerning an establishment so thoroughly well known. Mr. Coolidge is a native of the "Old Bay State" and inaugurated the enterprise in question forty years ago. He has been a member of the Marlboro board of selectmen for years, was representative in the Legislature for two years, and his services in advancing the best interests of the town are not easily overestimated for, aside from the powerful influence of his steadily developing business, he has done much to bring about the present prosperity of the community by his active co operation in all well-advised progressive movements and his determined opposition to such schemes as in his judgment were calculated to hamper or distort the town's growth. Of course, during his experience as a shoe manufacturer the business has undergone a radical change, hand labor has been largely dispensed with, and the tastes and demands of the public have been revolutionized, but Mr. Coolidge was never prone to adhere to bye-gone methods in the face of evident improvements, and the proof of this (if proof be needed) is to be found in his factory—one of the best equipped of the kind in the State. It is located at No. 25 Howland street, and is four stories in height and 36 × 200 feet in dimensions. Power is afforded by a twenty-five-horse engine, employment is given to 250 operatives, and the average production is 2500 pairs per day. Men's and boys' shoes, both light and heavy, are made, and considering the experience of the proprietor, and the unsurpassed facilities provided, it is hardly necessary to add that the product will bear the severest comparison with that of other factories, or that the heaviest orders can be filled at short notice and at the lowest market rates.

Lake Williams Ice Co., Marlboro, Mass.—Ice is no longer considered a luxury to be used only by the rich, but is conceded to be an actual necessity, the intelligent use of which will not only tend to neutralize the injurious effects of summer heat but will result in a saving being made in the cost of living, inasmuch as it preserves perishable food which would otherwise have to be thrown away. Therefore an abundant supply of ice of good quality is a positive boon to any community, and the residents of Marlboro have reason to congratulate themselves on being excellently served in this respect, for the Lake Williams Ice Company handle as pure and desirable a product as is to be found in the State, and quote prices that will bear the closest comparison with those named elsewhere. The enterprise was inaugurated about the year 1861, by J. W. Brigham, the existing stock company being organized in 1888. It is controlled entirely by Messrs. Ephraim, Irving, Winslow and Oscar Howe, these gentlemen having purchased all the stock held by other parties. Mr. Irving Howe acts as president, and Mr. Oscar Howe as treasurer. An extensive plant is maintained, the ice houses having sufficient capacity to accommodate a stock large enough to supply the most exceptional demand. During the season sixteen assistants are employed, and the service is so prompt and reliable as to be greatly appreciated by the community in general, family trade being given especially careful attention. Messrs. Ephraim Howe & Sons also carry on a large farm, including a valuable milk route, and in addition, do an extensive teaming business.

Geo. W. Rockwood, Carriage Painting and Varnishing, Middlesex Square, Marlboro, Mass.—The attention of our numerous readers is called to the enterprise of the above house which was founded some thirteen years ago, and at this stage of its existence, gives every indication of a permanent and profitable business. This enterprise was established in 1876, its present proprietor, Mr. Geo. W. Rockwood assuming full control in 1878, and the business premises occupied by him are located on Middlesex square, Marlboro, and cover an area of 2000 feet, where he possesses every facility for the prosecution of his industry, which consists of carriage painting in all its branches. Mr. Rockwood is thoroughly experienced in every detail of his trade and all orders are promptly attended to, perfect satisfaction is guaranteed in every particular. The extensive business requires the constant employment of skilled workmen, whose artistic tastes are displayed in the many fine specimens of work achieved by this house, and the work performed by Mr. Rockwood can in every way be depended on for durability, handsome finish, and tastefulness. Mr. Rockwood is a native of Charlton, Mass., and very well known in Marlboro and vicinity. He served as captain in the army for two years, and then re-enlisted in the artillery for one year. He is in all respects a thoroughly practical man exercising every care that nothing but the best workmanship shall emanate from his establishment, and we can rightly say that the reputation achieved by the work of his house serves as its best recommendation.

Wm. F. Hanlan, House, Sign and Decorative Painter; Shop corner Mechanic and Gay Streets, Marlboro, Mass.—Even ordinary house painting requires experience and care if satisfactory results are to be attained, and sign and decorative painting of course require a still higher degree of skill, for "cheap" looking signs or decorations are in the worst possible taste, and it is better to dispense with such altogether than to have anything but the best. The "best," however, is easy to get if discrimination be used in the placing of orders, and in this connection we may fittingly call attention to the character of the work done by Mr. Wm. F. Hanlan, for he has had long and varied experience in connection with the doing of house, sign and decorative painting, and we have no hesitation in guaranteeing satisfaction to all who may avail themselves of his services. Mr. Hanlan was born in Brookline, Mass., and began operations in Marlboro in 1886 as a member of the firm of Sandra & Hanlan, assuming sole control the same year. His shop is located on the corner of Mechanic and Gay streets, and is 25×40 feet in dimensions and supplied with all necessary facilities, etc. Employment is given to eight competent assistants, and orders can be filled at short notice, estimates being cheerfully given on large and small jobs. Among the specialties to which particular attention is given may be mentioned enamel painting, hard wood finishing, graining, glazing, etc., and we may add that care is taken to use the best of stock, thus assuring durable results.

Marlboro Rubber Company, wholesale and retail dealers in all kinds of Rubber Goods, under Windsor House, 218 Main Street, Marlboro.—Rubber is so unique a material that it is perfectly safe to say no substitute could be found for it were the supply to be cut off, while it is of such great and varied utility that despite the many uses that have already been made of it, new applications are constantly being brought forward. A comprehensive idea of its usefulness may be gained by visiting the store of the Marlboro Rubber Company, at No. 218 Main street, under the Windsor House, for the company deal in all kinds of rubber goods and carry a very extensive stock, comprising clothing for men's, women's, misses' and children's wear, rubber goods for medical purposes, boots, shoes, toys, foot balls, hose, packing, belting and other standard commodities, together with an exceptionally complete line of novelties and specialties of all kinds. The Rubber Company also carry the largest and finest line of umbrellas shown in any store in this part of the country. They also do a jobbing trade on rubber goods and umbrellas, and the retail dealers give them a good share of their stormy weather trade as well as their garden hose trade. The proprietor, Mr. A. F. Barnard, is a native of Orland, Maine, and was formerly with the Standard Rubber Company, largely engaged in the manufacture of rubber clothing of every description. He enjoys the most favorable relations with producers and is consequently in a position to quote bottom prices on all the goods handled, while those who have learned by experience how "uncertain" rubber goods are, will appreciate the fact that every article bought of the Marlboro Rubber Company is warranted to prove as represented.

Timothy Ryan & Co., dealers in Beef, Mutton, Lamb and Pork, at wholesale, corner Weed and Court Streets; Flour, Groceries and Provisions at retail, 7, 9 and 11 School Street, Marlboro, Mass.—The enterprise conducted by Messrs. Timothy Ryan & Co., was inaugurated about twenty years ago, having been founded by the senior partner of the present firm, Mr. Ryan did an exclusively retail business at first, but steadily increased the scope of his operations until now the firm of which he is head carry on one of the most extensive undertakings of the kind to be found in New England, outside the cities, and do a large and rapidly increasing wholesale business in beef, mutton, lamb and pork, in addition to their immense retail trade in groceries, flour and provisions in general. The retail store is located at Nos. 7, 9 and 11 School street, and has an area of 2000 square feet, while the wholesale establishment is at the corner of Weed and Court streets, and comprises two stories, each measuring 50 × 40 feet. Very extensive storage facilities for meats are here present, sufficient capacity being available to accommodate seventy-five cattle besides other meats. An immense stock is carried at both stores, and the assortment is as varied as it is large, for all classes of trade are catered to and all tastes and purses can easily be suited. The most satisfactory explanation of the success which has attended this enterprise is to be found in the fact that good faith has been kept with customers from the very beginning. When once the public learn that a certain dealer or a certain firm makes no announcements not justified by the facts, and is uniformly prepared to quote the lowest market rates on dependable goods, they are sure to give the undertaking cordial support and as this has ever been the policy pursued by the managers of the enterprise under consideration, its constant and rapid development is but a legitimate and natural result. The existing firm is constituted of Messrs. Timothy Ryan, A. W. Fitzgerald and T. J. Ryan, Jr., all of whom are widely known in Marlboro and vicinity. Employment is given to ten assistants, and both large and small orders are assured immediate and painstaking attention.

John J. Tracy, dealer in Harnesses, and manufacturer of the "Challenge" Harness, which is the best in the world for the money, 70 East Main Street, Marlborough, Mass.—When buying a harness it is well to remember the answer given by the Texan who was asked by a friend from the East if it was necessary to carry a revolver when in Texas, "Well," he replied, "you may carry a gun for a year without ever having occasion to use it, but when you do want one, you want it bad." So in using a harness you may get along with a poor and weakly made harness for a year or so all right, but when your horse takes fright, or anything else occurs to put an unusual strain on the rigging, you are very apt to come to grief and will be lucky if you escape with damage enough to pay for several harnesses. It is possible to get a thoroughly trustworthy article, at a moderate price, and you can prove this statement easily by calling at the establishment conducted by Mr. John J. Tracy, at No. 70 East Main Street, and learn his prices.

This gentleman makes harnesses to order that will stand every reasonable test to which they can be put, and offers his goods at prices that are bound to suit. Business was begun here by Mr. Tracy in 1886. He is a native of Waltham, Mass., and is well known throughout this vicinity. One floor of the dimensions of 300 square feet is utilized for the harness business, and an additional storehouse for other goods. Harnesses of all kinds and styles, including the famous "Challenge" harness, which is the best in the world for the money, are made and dealt in, and repairing is neatly and durably done. New and second-hand wagons and sleighs are dealt in, and Mr. Tracy is also agent for the Mica Axle Grease, which is conceded to be the best in the world.

Fitch & Foster, dealers in Choice Groceries, Meats, Provisions, Butter, Cheese, Fresh Eggs, Foreign and Domestic Fruits, 57 Main Street, Marlboro, Mass.—Messrs. Fitch & Foster have carried on their present store at No. 57 Main street since 1888, having at that date succeeded Messrs. Allen & Jordan. The establishment deserves especially favorable mention for a number of reasons, prominent among which are the magnitude and variety of the stock carried, the quality of the goods handled, the uniform fairness of the prices quoted and the accommodating spirit manifested by the management. Messrs. E. H. Fitch and W. Foster are both natives of Nova Scotia, and that they fully understand their business in every detail is shown by the many advantages they are enabled to offer their customers. Choice staple and fancy groceries, meats, provisions, and foreign and domestic fruits are extensively dealt in, together with a full line of selected country produce, such as butter, cheese, fresh eggs, etc. The firm cater expressly to family trade, and by obtaining their supplies from the most reputable sources are enabled to fully guarantee that every article sold shall prove as represented. Sufficient assistance is employed to ensure prompt attention to every caller, and large and small buyers are given equal consideration at all times.

Marlboro Steam Laundry, Established in 1878, William H. Osgood, proprietor, 232 Main Street, Marlboro, Mass.—During the twelve years that the Marlboro Steam Laundry has been in operation, the public have had ample opportunity to form a deliberate and intelligent opinion as to whether it "pays" to send goods to a public laundry or not, and the verdict rendered is plainly indicated by the fact that the patronage has steadily increased and still continues to do so. The enterprise was inaugurated by Mr. W. A. Arnold, who was succeeded by Mr. M. M. Walter, he giving place, in 1886, to Mr. J. T. Wheeler, who in 1888 became associated with Mr. Leslie M. Frye, and in 1889 Mr. Wm. H. Osgood assumed control. Mr. Osgood is a native of Peabody, Mass. He gives that careful personal attention to the supervision of affairs so essential to the keeping up of the service to the highest standard of efficiency. The laundry is located in Mechanics' square, the office being at No. 232 Main street. The facilities at hand are of the most improved description, enabling the extensive business to be easily handled, while the system in operation is so carefully considered and thoroughly carried out that errors occurring from the loss or exchange of articles are reduced to a minimum. Employment is given to twenty assistants, and it is worthy of note that all ladies' wear is entirely under the charge of lady help—a policy that is appreciated by patrons. A team will call for goods when desired, and as work is delivered in the same way, customers merely have to prepare the bundle for the driver, he calling for and delivering it without extra charge. Mr. Osgood has also added a carpet cleaning department which is giving great satisfaction to the people of Marlboro and vicinity. Carpets are collected and thoroughly renovated at short notice and satisfaction guaranteed.

Central House, F. E. Brooks, Proprietor,

Marlboro, Mass.—The Central House was opened a number of years ago and has been carried on by many different proprietors, coming under the control of Mr. S. F. Barden in 1885, who was succeeded by Mr. F. E. Brooks, the present proprietor, in June, 1887. This gentleman was already well and favorably known to the travelling public, in connection with the Old Colony House of South Framingham, which he built in 1882, and has since carried on in a manner which has given it a much more than local reputation. The Central House has been newly fitted and refurnished throughout, and is now one of the best-equipped hotels to be found in the State, outside the larger cities. It has steam heat and electric light, and the comfort and convenience of guests are carfully provided for in every respect. The central location of the house, at No. 130 Main street, renders its name a most appropriate one, and aside from the superior accommodations offered, would serve to make it a favorite with commercial travellers and others whose time is of value. Employment is given to nine assistants, and the promptness and accuracy of the service is a very popular feature of the management. The table is supplied with well-cooked and substantial food, and the bill of fare is varied enough to allow of all tastes being suited. Accommodations can be furnished to fifty guests, and as the terms are very reasonable, considering the service provided, it is not surprising that the Central House should always be well patronized.

Frank Gauvin, wholesale and retail dealer in

Choice Groceries, Provisions, Fruit, Vegetables, Poultry, Bread, Cake and Pastry, Grain, Hay and Straw, etc.; also dealer in Boots, Shoes and Rubbers, 241 and 243 Lincoln Street, Marlboro, Mass.—One of the most attractive establishments in town is that of which Mr. Frank Gauvin is the proprietor, located at Nos. 241 and 243 Lincoln street. This establishment was founded about twenty years ago, business having been begun by Mr. Gauvin in 1861, who has since built up so large and thriving a business, which is both wholesale and retail in character, as to prove that his goods and prices are as popular as his store is attractive. Mr. Gauvin was born in Canada, and is very well and favorably known throughout Marlboro. The premises occupied by Mr. Gauvin comprise a store 30 X 50 feet, and a bakery. His store is stocked with a varied assortment of goods including choice groceries, provisions, fresh and salt meats, fruits, vegetables, poultry, bread, cake and pastry, flour, teas and coffees; also grain, hay, straw, etc. Mr. Gauvin has a department devoted to the sale of boots, shoes and rubbers, and offers some decided inducements to customers in this line of goods. Three efficient assistants are constantly employed, and all customers are assured prompt attention and equitable treatment. Mr. Gauvin is able to offer some superior advantages in the way of freshness and general desirability of the various articles he handles, and in every instance warrants all goods leaving his establishment to prove as represented. Orders are accurately delivered and no avoidable delay permitted.

E. F. Longley, Wooden Boxes, Job Planing

and Sawing, Knife Grinding, etc., Marlboro Mass.—Competition is very close and keen nowadays in about every line of manufacture, and it does not require a very decided advantage to turn the scale in favor of any given enterprise, so that it is perfectly reasonable to say that the undertaking conducted by Mr. E. F. Longley is an important factor in making Marlboro a prominent shoe manufacturing centre, for Mr. Longley is extensively engaged in the production of shoe boxes and sells them direct to manufacturers, at the very lowest prevailing rates. He has a most thoroughly equipped establishment, and is prepared to fill the most extensive orders at very short notice. The business is not confined to this special feature by any means, for it includes the making of wooden boxes in general, as well as the doing of job planing and sawing, knife grinding, etc. The factory is located on Manning street, and has an area of 5930 square feet. It is fitted up with a complete plant of woodworking machinery, and employment is given to fifteen assistants. The business was formerly carried on by Mr. Joseph Manning, but since 1885, has been under the control of the present proprietor, who is a native of Boylston, Mass., and is very generally known in this vicinity.

Charles J. Magrath, dealer in Wall Paper,

Mouldings, Window Shades, etc., etc., Hazelton Block, 199 Main Street, Marlboro, Mass.—The well-known establishment of Chas. J. Magrath, located at No. 199 Main street, was founded in 1889, and since that date has been under the able management of Mr. Magrath excepting about three months when it was under the management of Harding & Appleton. It has already attained to a position of prominence among the leading retail houses of Marlboro. The premises occupied for business purposes cover an area of 475 square feet. The magnitude and variety of the stock carried is at all times prepared for the demand upon it, and embraces a large assortment and variety of wall paper, window shades, draperies, poles, mouldings, etc. Mr. Magrath makes it a point to carry only the most reliable goods, and such as he can confidently recommend to his customers. The assortments are full and choice, and very low prices are quoted. It is without doubt one of the best stores of its kind in Marlboro, and is conducted on strict business principles. Mr. Magrath is a native of Greenwich, Mass., and is thoroughly conversant with his business in all its details. He is an energetic and progressive gentleman of integrity and personal worth who enjoys a large patronage throughout this community.

A. B. Howe & Co., dealers in all kinds of Lumber, Doors, Sashes, Blinds, etc., Florence Street, near Old Colony Depot, Marlboro, Mass. —There is naturally a great deal of lumber and other building material consumed annually in a rapidly growing community such as Marlboro, and the facilities for obtaining such commodities in any desired quantities at moderate rates is a matter of general interest. Among those firms which have done much to bring about the present desirable condition of things in the local lumber business, prominent mention should rightfully be made of Messrs. A. B. Howe & Co., for this concern have carried on operations for about nine years, and have the reputation of furnishing strictly dependable goods at the very lowest market rates. The partners are Messrs. A. B. and G. A. Howe, both of whom were born in Marlboro and are universally known throughout this vicinity. Mr G. A. Howe served in the army during the Rebellion, and is at present connected with the board of selectmen. The premises made use of are located on Florence street, near the Old Colony Depot, and comprise several spacious storehouses A very large stock is constantly carried, consisting of lumber, doors, sash, blinds, etc., and employment is given to nine assistants. All orders, whether large or small, being assured immediate and painstaking attention. Messrs. A. B. Howe & Co. enjoy the most favorable relations with manufacturers and quote bottom prices.

L. O. Cunningham, dealer in Provisions, Main Street, Marlboro, Mass.—The handling of strictly first class goods, the extension of courteous treatment to every customer, and the maintenance of fair and reasonable prices in every department, are reasons for giving a business enterprise specially prominent mention, then we can do no less than to take this course with that conducted by Mr. L. O. Cunningham, located at No. 24 Main street, Marlboro, for this gentleman manages his undertaking in precisely the manner indicated, and warrants every article purchased of him shall prove precisely as represented. It is hardly necessary for us to state that his business is a large retail one, for it is not everywhere that purchasers can be so positively assured of getting the full worth of their money and this fact is very generally appreciated and acted upon. The premises utilized cover an area of 800 square feet. Those wishing the choicest meats, provisions, vegetables, fruits, etc., have no occasion to go beyond the limits of Mr. Cunningham's establishment to find the same as a specialty is made of catering to this class of trade and particular attention is paid to the procuring of supplies of such a superior character that they cannot fail to give perfect satisfaction. Competent and courteous assistants are employed, and every order will be given prompt and painstaking attention. This establishment was originally founded by Marshall Dadmun, who was succeeded by Messrs. Willard & Cunningham in 1878, Mr. L. O. Cunningham assuming entire control of the business in 1879. He is a native of Marlboro, and served in the army over three and one-half years during our late civil war. He is well known in this community, and highly respected as an honorable business man.

C. L. Bartlett, successor to S. A. Houghton, Domestic Bakery. Orders left at Bread Store, 101 Main Street, will receive Prompt Attention. East Main opposite Church Street, Marlboro, Mass.—Sta'e bread may be very healthy eating, as the doctors would have us believe, but the vast majority of people prefer theirs fresh, and this is a very fortunate thing for the bakers, as otherwise their business would be decidedly diminished. Not a few families use baker's bread that would content themselves with the home made article could they have it fresh daily, and it is noticeable that those bakeries are most popular where the stock is the most often renewed, and is consequently the freshest. This goes far to explain the warm reception which has been given the Domestic Bakery, now conducted by Mr. C. L. Bartlett, and located on East Main street, opposite Church street. This bakery was established in 1882, by Mr. S. A. Houghton, who was succeeded by the present proprietor in 1884. Mr. Bartlett does an extensive business both wholesale and retail in character. Special attention is given to the retail trade, and all orders left at the Bread Store at No. 101 Main street, will receive prompt attention. Four competent assistants are constantly employed, and the proprietor makes it a point to offer only fresh and palatable goods to his customers, thus it is but natural that the popularity we have alluded to should have been won. Mr. Bartlett is a native of Norwich, Vt., and well known in the vicinity of Marlboro, where he deals in about everything usually handled at a first class and thoroughly reliable bakery.

Treacy Bros., dealers in Boots, Shoes, Slippers, Rubbers and Rubber Boots, Blacking and Shoe Dressing, Boot and Shoe Repairing a Specialty, 150 Main Street, Marlboro, Mass.— The best cure for corns that is in the market to day, is a well fitting pair of boots or shoes, made from soft and pliable stock, and if this simple fact was generally known and acted upon, there would be a sudden drop in the demand for "corn plasters," "corn salves," etc., which are generally all very well in their way, but which cannot accomplish miracles or eradicate corns while the cause of their growth still remains. Messrs. Treacy Bros. carry a large stock of good, comfortable foot wear, and their assortment of shapes and sizes is so large that a fit can be confidently promised to patrons, while the goods are fully warranted to prove as represented and are quoted at bottom prices, from slippers to brogans. The store is located at No. 150 Main street and is of the dimensions of 22×75 feet, and is well and favorably known to the public, being a store whose reputation is of the highest type. It was established in the spring of 1887 by Messrs. John and Andrew M. Treacy, who are both natives of Marlboro. This firm handle boots, shoes, slippers, rubbers and rubber boots, and offer many of the latest novelties in these lines as well as an exceptionally full selection of the more staple styles for ladies', gents' and children's wear. Blacking and shoe dressing are also dealt in, and boot and shoe repairing is made a specialty and guaranteed to be done in the most satisfactory manner both as regards style of work and prices charged.

E. M. Estabrook, dealer in Fine Family Groceries, Choice Teas, Coffees and Spices; Best Brands of Haxoll and St. Louis Flours; High Grades of Creamery Butter a Specialty, corner Lincoln and Mechanic Streets (Carter's Block), Marlboro, Mass.—Everybody is familiar with the fact that some people can live comfortably on an income that others would starve on, and of course everybody knows that this is chiefly owing to superior methods of management. There is an art of buying as well as an art of selling, and many intelligent individuals never seem to learn that in order to buy to the best advantage, it is necessary to pick out a reputable and reliable house and deal with it entirely, as long as the results are satisfactory. Since Mr. E. M. Estabrook founded the undertaking which is conducted by him at the corner of Lincoln and Mechanic streets, he has built up a thriving retail trade and many of his best customers are to be ranked among the most careful and discriminating class of buyers. Business was begun in 1888, and family supplies have been made a specialty from the first. The premises occupied cover an area of 1500 square feet and an extensive stock is carried, consisting of fine staple and fancy groceries, choice teas, coffees, and spices; also the best brands of Haxall and St. Louis flours, and high grades of creamery butter is made a specialty. The favor which this enterprise has met, is largely due to the prompt and polite attention that is given to all orders, and the efficient assistants in attendance will be found active and willing in the discharge of their duties at all times. All goods handled by Mr. Estabrook are of standard quality and are offered at prices that will ensure a constant renewal of the stock.

Adams & Crocker, wholesale and retail dealers in Hardware, Paints, Oils and Varnishes, Agricultural Implements and Shoe Kit, special terms to Builders, No. 148 Main Street, Marlboro, Mass.—The business conducted by Messrs. Adams & Crocker was founded a number of years ago by Mr. John M. Whiton, Jr., and was continued in 1884 by Messrs. Whiton & Putnam, this firm being succeeded in 1886, by Mr. C. F. Whitney, who gave place to the present proprietors in 1887. Mr. Bert J. Adams is a native of this town, and Mr. Charles E. Crocker was born in West Hanover, Mass. The firm do an extensive business, it having developed largely of late years, and are prepared to fill either wholesale or retail orders at the very lowest market rates. Among the leading commodities handled may be mentioned hardware, paints, oils and varnishes, of which a heavy and varied stock is carried, comprising the productions of the most reputable manufacturers. Special terms are made to builders, and this fact, together with the promptness and accuracy with which orders are filled, has resulted in the building up of a very large trade in this department alone. Agricultural implements and shoe kit are also dealt in largely, and a fine line of whips and horse furnishings in general is constantly on hand to select from. The store occupies one floor and a basement, of the dimensions of 24 × 65 feet, and is located at No. 148 Main street. Employment is given to two assistants, and callers are assured immediate and courteous attention.

C. L. Bliss, manufacturer of Cigars of all kinds; Private Brands made to order, Marlboro, Mass.—The statements that have been made from time to time concerning the methods practiced by the "tenement house" cigar makers of New York and other large cities, have had their effect on the general public, and the consequence is that retailers find it for their interest to obtain goods from sources beyond suspicion. Experienced smokers also know that the enjoyment to be derived from a cigar is as directly dependent upon its making as upon the quality of the tobacco used, and hence place their orders with dealers who handle the product of skilled labor. The increasing popularity of "private brands" is largely due to the fact that these are apt to be more uniform in quality than are ordinary goods, and as on the uniformity of a brand its success is chiefly dependent, those putting such on the market would do well to avail themselves of the facilities offered by Mr. C. L. Bliss, as he makes a specialty of the manufacture of private brands to order and is prepared to execute all commissions at short notice and in a thoroughly satisfactory manner. Mr. Bliss was born in Taunton, Mass., and began operations in Marlboro in 1872. His establishment is located at No. 119 East Main street, where premises having an area of 22×50 square feet are occupied, and employment is given to twenty competent assistants. Particular attention is paid to handwork and no pains is spared to fully maintain the enviable reputation now held among the trade. Mr. Bliss has recently completed a fine new shop at the rear of his dwelling, to be used entirely for manufacturing. It is two stories in height and measures 42×30 feet. Mr. Bliss's former factory, which is located close by being used exclusively for storage purposes.

Alex. Scott, dealer in Groceries, Meat, Bread, Provisions and Canned Goods, 296 Lincoln Street, Marlboro, Mass.—It would be an unaccountable and unpardonable omission if we were to make no mention of the establishment of Mr. Alex. Scott in this review of Marlboro's business enterprises, for the undertaking alluded to was founded about nine years ago, business having been begun in 1881. Mr. Scott is a native of Canada and as a matter of course has hosts of friends in Marlboro and vicinity, not only on account of his long residence here and business prominence, but also by reason of the office he holds as Justice of the Peace. The store occupied covers an area of 21×65 feet, the whole amount of this space being required to accommodate the very heavy stock carried, which includes full lines of fine groceries, meats, bread and provisions. Mr. Scott's experience and the favorable relations established with producers, wholesalers, etc., during his long and honorable business career enables him to quote very low rates on the articles he handles, as well as to fully guarantee that they shall prove strictly as represented. Employing four competent and polite assistants, he is in a position to extend prompt and courteous service to all, and it is therefore not surprising that a large and steadily increasing retail business should be done. Mr. Scott for eight years previous to his present business conducted a bakery which he was also very successful in.

D. A. Walker & Co., Groceries, Flour and Grain, Canned Goods, Creamery Butter a Specialty, 160 Main Street, Marlboro, Mass.—The leading position that has long been held by the enterprise carried on by Messrs. D. A. Walker & Co., entitles it to very prominent mention in any review of Marlboro's representative business undertakings, and it is certainly an agreeable duty to chronicle the success of this widely-known firm, for their extensive business has been built up by the employment of strictly legitimate methods, and by sparing no trouble to offer the most efficient service that circumstances would allow. The enterprise had its inception in 1874, the firm style of H. Belknap & Co., consisting of H. Belknap, and D. A. Walker, this firm being succeeded in 1889 by D. A. Walker, D. A. Archibald, and F. T. Curtis, the present firm. Both Messrs. Walker and Curtis being natives of this State, Mr. Archibald being a native of Nova Scotia. This firm have a large circle of friends throughout Marlboro and vicinity. The premises utilized, comprise one floor and a basement, and are 22 × 76 feet in dimensions, affording ample room for the accommodation of a large and varied stock, embracing choice staple and fancy groceries, fine teas and coffees, and pure spices, canned goods, flour and grain, etc. All the commodities dealt in are carefully selected with a special view to the requirements of family trade, but particular attention is paid to the handling of choice creamery butter, no finer grades being obtainable in the market than those offered at this popular store. The prices rule very low in every department of the business, and as employment is given to four efficient assistants, every caller may depend upon receiving prompt and polite attention.

Arnaud Brothers, dealers in Fresh, Salt, Smoked and Pickled Fish, Oysters, Clams, Scallops, etc., No. 18 Main Street (next to the "Brick Store,") Marlboro, Mass.—A store where a good many things are sold, and where the stock carried is remarkable for excellence not less than for variety, is that of which Messrs. Arnaud Brothers and J. A. Wheeler are the proprietors, located at No. 18 Main street (next to the Brick Block). Business was started here in 1886, and whatever popularity the enterprise has won (and that is by no means inconsiderable), has been gained by hard work and a determination to furnish the best of goods at the lowest possible prices. The premises in use measure 20 × 90 feet and afford ample accommodations for the heavy stock that is constantly kept on hand. Among the articles dealt in may be mentioned, fresh, salt, smoked and pickled fish, oysters, clams, scallops, etc. The individual members of this firm are Messrs. Frank R., and J. C. Arnaud, and Mr. J. A. Wheeler, all of whom are natives of Wellfleet, Mass., and are highly respected, as energetic and reliable business men in Marlboro. One thing is particularly noticeable in connection with their store, and that is, that misrepresentation is never *knowingly* practised in the slightest degree. It is the desire of the firm that every customer shall know just what he is buying and just what he is getting for his money, and it is no fault of the management if this knowledge is not always had. Celerity and courtesy are extended to callers.

H. A. Spalding, Blacksmith and Wheelwright, Horse Shoeing and General Jobbing, all kinds of Carriage Work to order, corner Mechanic and Lincoln Streets, Marlborough, Mass.—The business carried on by Mr. H. A. Spalding was founded over forty years ago by Mr. William E. Brigham, who was succeeded by Messrs. Maynard & Spalding in 1887, the present proprietor assuming sole control the same year. He is a native of New Ipswich, N. H., and by careful personal attention to the details of his business has fully maintained the leading position so long held by the enterprise with which he is now identified. The premises occupied are located on the corner of Mechanic and Lincoln streets, and comprise a main shop, three stories in height and 50×60 feet in dimensions, and a one story ell measuring 25×35 feet. They are equipped with the most improved facilities for the doing of blacksmithing, wheelwrighting, horse-shoeing and general jobbing, and all kinds of carriage work will be done to order at short notice and in a thoroughly satisfactory manner. Mr. Spalding employs five efficient assistants, and gives particular attention to repairing, the work being promptly, neatly and durably done at moderate rates. A heavy and complete stock of carriages is constantly carried, embracing vehicles of the most stylish and approved designs, and the very lowest prices are quoted, while every carriage is guaranteed to prove just as represented.

Gleason House, James M. Gleason & Son, Proprietors, 71-79 Main Street, Marlboro, Mass.—The kind of hotel one prefers depends a good deal of course upon individual tastes, for some persons think more of style than they do of comfort and choose their hotel accordingly, but the large majority of travelers take a different view of the subject and prefer to put up where they can feel entirely at home. It is not easy to find a really "home-like" hotel, for by no means all that claim to be such are what they profess to be, but it is worth while taking some little trouble to hunt one up, although we propose to save our readers that work so far as Marlboro is concerned at any rate, by calling their attention to the Gleason House, located at Nos. 71-79 Main street, for if ever there was a hotel where the management really strove to make guests feel at home it is the one in question. Operations were begun in 1885, and the house has already attained an enviable reputation, especially among commercial travelers, to whom special rates are made. Some fifty guests can be accommodated at one time, and the sleeping rooms, beds, etc., are kept in first-class condition, a fact that will be appreciated by the many who have suffered from the carelessness practiced in this respect at some of the most pretentious hotels in New England. Employment is given to eight competent assistants, and prompt attention and courtesy are assured to all guests, the management insisting upon this, and taking pains to see that it is duly attended to. A billiard hall, bath-room, barber shop, etc., are connected with the hotel, and in short all modern conveniences are provided for patrons. The proprietors are Messrs. James M. Gleason & Son, both of whom are natives of Marlboro, and have a very extensive circle of friends throughout this section.

C. H. Stone, dealer in Flour, Grain and Groceries, Canned Goods, etc., 140 Main Street, Marlboro, Mass.—It is not far from a score of years since the enterprise now carried on by Mr. C. H. Stone was inaugurated, for it was started in 1871 by Messrs. John Stone & Co., the present proprietor being a member of the original firm and assuming sole control in 1879. He is a native of Northboro, Mass., and is universally known throughout this section, having been a member of the Board of Selectmen for five years, and being prominent and active in advancing the best interests of the community. Mr. Stone deals very extensively in flour, grain and groceries, and unquestionably enjoys as desirable a family trade as any dealer in this section of the State, for he has always catered to this class of patrons and spares no pains to supply goods that will give the best of satisfaction to the most critical. The store utilized by him is located at No. 140 Main street, and comprises one floor and a basement of the dimensions of 22×60 feet, besides a spacious storehouse. Employment is given to two competent and courteous assistants, and callers are waited on promptly and carefully at all times. Mr. Stone handles the most popular brands of flour, and is prepared to quote bottom prices on this commodity in large or small lots. Grain, feed, etc., are also dealt in largely, and the stock of fancy and staple groceries offered is worthy of especial commendation, for it is exceptionally complete in every department, is made up of strictly dependable articles, and includes one of the most desirable assortments of canned goods to be found in this vicinity.

G. A. Spofford, dealer in Stationery, Cigars, Tobacco, Fruit, Confectionery, Bread, Cake, Pastry, etc., Forest Hall Block, corner Lincoln and Winthrop Streets, Marlboro, Mass.—It is an excellent idea to use fine stationery in social correspondence, for the expense of doing so is really trifling, and there is no way in which respect for one's correspondents can be more unobtrusively and yet effectively shown. There are many beautiful novelties in this line of goods now on the market, and one of the best places to examine and purchase such is at the store carried on by Mr. George A. Spofford, located in Forest Hall Block, corner of Lincoln and Winthrop streets. Mr. Spofford is a Wayland, Mass., man by birth, and assumed control of the establishment to which we have reference in 1889. He served in the army four years and has many friends in Marlboro and vicinity. The establishment under question was originally established by Mr. C. L. Russell, who was succeeded by Mr. H. D. Barker in 1887, the present proprietor, having succeeded the latter in 1889. Premises of the dimensions of 30 × 40 feet are occupied, and the stock on hand includes the usual variety of goods to be found in a first class store of this kind. All the leading styles in stationery and stationer's articles are dealt in, beside a good stock of toys are carried in stock. Also first-class fruits and confectionery, ice cream, soda, cigars, tobacco and canned goods of all kinds, and bread, cake, and pastry, is received fresh every day. Mr. Spofford's prices are very reasonable in each department, and visitors to this establishment will find a choice variety of goods to select from.

J. A. Andrews & Co., Contractor and Builder, General Carpenter Work, Florence Street, Marlboro, Mass.—It is a noteworthy fact that while some men seem to take genuine pleasure in building, others go through such trials and tribulations when erecting a house as to discourage them from ever repeating the experiment. The explanation of this is to be found in the difference in the methods adopted, for the class of men first referred to take pains to entrust the carrying out of their projects to competent and responsible contractors, while those who are always "in trouble," have in the majority of cases, been careless in this important respect. There are enough good builders to make it easy to find a suitable firm, and among those carrying on operations in this vicinity, prominent mention should be made of Messrs. J. A. Andrews & Co., for this concern is made up of honorable and experienced men and has a high record for competency and integrity. The firm was formed two years ago, the partners being Messrs. J. A. and Geo. J. Andrews, both of whom are natives of this town. The shop is located on Florence street, and has an area of about 1000 square feet. Employment is given to sixteen assistants, this force being largely increased when occasion requires. Estimates will be promptly and cheerfully made on receipt of plans and specifications, and the firm are prepared to figure closely on carpentering and building of every description. General jobbing is also given immediate and careful attention, satisfactory work being done at moderate rates.

Alvin Wheeler, dealer in Groceries, Provisions, etc., 192 Main Street, Marlboro, Mass.—Many a housekeeper has said when she discovered that the goods sent to her were not what were ordered or were unsatisfactory in some other respect, "Oh I wish I could find a grocery and provision dealer who could be entirely relied upon," and it is just this information that we propose to supply in the present article and therefore respectfully call the attention of our many readers to the enterprise now conducted by A. Wheeler, who is a native of Massachusetts. This house was originally established by Mr. E. L. Green who was succeeded by A. C. Taylor & Co., in 1886, and in April, 1889, Mr. Wheeler assumed control, and its record since that date, has been such as to entitle its proprietor to the entire confidence of the public. The establishment under question is located at No. 192 Main street, and covers an area of 25 × 42 feet containing an extensive assortment of groceries and provisions carefully selected for family trade, among which will be found at all times fine meats, groceries, canned goods, fruit and vegetables. Three competent assistants are employed and customers are served promptly, politely, honestly, and in short satisfactorily. This house makes a specialty of filling orders accurately and promptly, and may be relied upon to earnestly strive to furnish customers with such goods as are sure to prove desirable. Much of the large retail business, now done by Mr. Wheeler, is due to his practice in this respect, and housekeepers will save themselves much worry and disappointment by establishing business relations with a house of this character. Prices quoted here are low and all seasonable goods are kept in stock.

J. Gregoire, Fashionable Millinery, Dry and Fancy Goods, also Human Hair Goods, 254 and 256 Lincoln Street, Marlboro, Mass.—A very popular establishment indeed is that conducted by Mrs. J. Gregoire and Mr. Jonas Gregoire at Nos. 254 and 256 Lincoln street, and during the years that the enterprise in question has been carried on, it has become more and more evident to discriminating buyers that the advantages here offered were hard to parallel elsewhere. This establishment was founded in 1880 by the above firm, millinery and human hair goods being then the principal goods carried, and in 1887 dry and fancy goods were added. The store utilized by the above firm measures 52×22 feet, and the stock of goods carried is so complete and varied that even to catalogue it would more than exhaust all our available space, and after all would not begin to give an adequate idea of what it really comprises. The proprietors are thoroughly acquainted with the many details of their business, and spare no pains to accommodate customers in the most liberal and superior manner for which their establishment has long been noted. This firm offer a fine assortment of dry goods, millinery and human hair goods, that is both seasonable and fashionable, and the extensive business done requires the services of five assistants in the busy season. We therefore commend this establishment to our readers in particular, and the public in general, and are assured that all patrons will be served in a courteous and liberal manner.

Marlboro Dye House, R. W. Geddes, proprietor. Established 1880, No. 8 Liberty Street, Marlboro.—A great deal of clothing is thrown aside as "worn out" when, as a matter of fact, it is not worn out at all, the fabric being about as whole and sound as ever, but the appearance of the garments being spoiled by grease or other dirt or by the effects of the sun. Now, there is no reason why money should be thrown away in this fashion, while such an establishment as the Marlboro Dye House is in operation, for every facility is at hand here to cleanse, dye and re-finish ladies' and gentlemen's garments by the most approved methods, and orders are filled at short notice and moderate rates. This enterprise was inaugurated in 1880 and has been carried on in a liberal and accommodating manner that has made it very popular, not only among the residents of Marlboro, but also throughout this section, for orders sent by express will receive equally prompt and careful attention as those delivered in person. Goods left by Tuesday will be finished the latter part of the same week, and no trouble is spared to attain results that will give the best of satisfaction. The Dye House has an area of about 1000 square feet and is located at No. 8 Liberty street. Office hours are from 7.30 A. M. to 6 P. M., and Tuesday and Saturday evenings from 6.30 to 8 o'clock, and all callers are assured prompt and polite attention. The proprietor, Mr. R. W. Geddes, is a native of East Greenwich, R. I., and understands his business thoroughly in every detail, having served an apprenticeship of four years and has been a practical dyer for fourteen years. Competent assistance is employed, and the work turned out will bear the closest examination and comparison with that done elsewhere.

John M. Carpenter, dealer in Fine Ready-Made Clothing, Hats, Caps, etc., etc., Phoenix Block, Main Street, Marlboro, Mass.—The genial gentleman whose card we print above ranks among the best known and most highly esteemed of our Marlboro business men and fully deserves the success he has won in the carrying on of his present enterprise. The establishment now conducted by Mr. John M. Carpenter was founded in 1885 by Mr. Geo. H. Palmer, who was succeeded in 1886 by Messrs. John M. Carpenter & Co., the present proprietor having assumed full control of the business in 1888, and has built up a large retail business during the comparatively short time that he has conducted the industry in question. This is not surprising when his methods are taken into consideration, for everybody likes fair dealing, everybody likes courteous treatment, everybody likes fashionable and thoroughly made garments, and everybody likes to secure a first class article at a moderate price. All these likings can be and are satisfied by Mr. Carpenter, and his popularity follows as a matter of course. Mr. John M. Carpenter is a native of Milford, Mass., and is very well known throughout Marlboro. At his establishment, located in Phoenix Block, Main street, he always carries in stock a fine assortment of ready-made clothing, hats, caps, etc., etc., embracing goods suited to all conditions of wear. The premises occupied comprise a store 24 × 70 feet in dimensions, and employment is given to two reliable and courteous assistants. Mr. Carpenter makes a specialty of carrying all the latest styles in stock, and satisfaction is guaranteed to every customer, and his experience has thus far been that those who patronize him once, almost invariably come again. His prices are extremely low for first-class garments, and we can commend his goods to the most fastidious dressers.

William Barnes, Life and Fire Insurance Agent, Real Estate Agent, Conveyancer, Negotiator of Mortgages, Office 156 Main Street, Marlborough, Mass.—Among those identified with insurance and real estate matters in Marlborough and vicinity, Mr. William Barnes must be given a leading position, for this gentleman has carried on operations here for a full score of years and has long been recognized as an authority in these special lines. He served two years in the army during the Rebellion and began business in Marlborough in 1869. Mr. Barnes has an office in Week's Block, No. 156 Main street, and those seeking information relative to insurance or real estate matters will find him ready to give any assistance in his power, while mail communications addressed to post office box 856, will also receive immediate and careful attention. He represents some of the most popular and most trustworthy insurance companies in the world, and is in a position to write life, fire and accident policies at the lowest market rates. We take pleasure in presenting the following list of corporations, for which Mr. Barnes is authorized to act, for we believe it to be unsurpassed by that shown by any agent in this section of the State, and we know that those placing insurance through this office will be assured honorable and liberal treatment in every respect:

First National Insurance Co., Worcester; Merchants' & Farmers' Insurance Co., Worcester;

Worcester Mutual Fire Insurance Co., Worcester; Citizens' Mutual Fire Insurance Co., Boston; Westchester Fire Insurance Co., New York City; Commercial Union Assurance Co., London, England; Guardian Assurance Corporation, London, England; Phoenix Assurance Co., London, England; Northern Assurance Co., London and Aberdeen; London Assurance Corporation, London; Western Assurance Co., Toronto, Canada; St. Paul Fire & Marine Insurance Co., Minn.; Travellers's Life and Accident, Hartford, Conn.

First National Bank, 38 Mechanics Street, Marlboro.—During the comparatively few years which the First National Bank has been in existence, it has attained a leading position among the financial institutions of this section, and as it has been said that " confidence is a plant of slow growth," it may be of interest to trace out some of the reasons why its growth has been so rapid in connection with the bank in question. The first, and unquestionably the main explanation, is to be found in the character and standing of those who inaugurated and conduct the enterprise. The fact that all of them are manufacturers or merchants doing business in Marlboro, not only furnishes the best possible assurance that they have the material interests of the community at heart, but also gives them the advantage of personal acquaintance with the majority of those having occasion to use the facilities the bank affords, and it may be stated right here that these facilities are very extensive. The institution has a capital of $150,000, and enjoys favorable relations with correspondents throughout the country. Money will be forwarded to any part of the world, and particular attention is paid to collections in the United States and Canada, very favorable terms being quoted. All business entrusted to the bank is assured immediate and painstaking attention, and the invariable policy of the management is to give equally careful consideration to large and small customers —a fact going far to explain its popularity with business men in general. Other things being equal, the preference is always given to local enterprises when the question of affording financial aid comes up, and we need hardly say that such timely assistance may often be the means of avoiding embarrassment if not total failure which would seriously interfere with the town's development. The following is a list of the officers, and we may safely leave it for our readers to decide whether what we have said concerning them is justified by the facts or not:

President : Wm. H. Fay.
Cashier ; F. L. Claflin.
Directors : W. H. Fay, Wm. Morse, Edward F. Johnson, Chas. L. Fay, Geo. N. Cate, T. A. Coolidge, W. A. Alley.

O'Brien & Conry, Staple and Fancy Groceries, Dried and Pickled Fish, Crockery, Glass and Wooden Ware, etc., 151 Main Street, Marlboro, Mass.—When we say that the grocery store carried on by Messrs. O'Brien & Conry at No. 151 Main street, Marlboro, is worthy of liberal patronage, we perhaps should also give our reasons for making this assertion, for an unsupported statement cannot be expected to carry a great deal of weight and it is perfectly natural for intelligent people to want to know why a thing

is so as well as that it *is* so. Prominent among the good points of this establishment is the character of the stock it contains. This stock is choice, varied and fresh. It has been carefully chosen from the goods offered by the foremost wholesalers of the State and will compare favorably with that of any other strictly retail store. It includes staple and fancy groceries, teas, coffees and spices, canned goods, flour, foreign and domestic fruits, butter, eggs and cheese, dried and pickled fish, crockery, glass and woolen ware, etc. Special care has been taken in the selection of the teas and coffees carried in stock, both as regards their wholesomeness and their purity. The fine line of flour offered is also worthy of special mention, for it is made up of brands particularly adapted to family use, and is sold at the very lowest market rates. We might also call attention to the character of the fine assortment of crockery, glass and wooden ware offered, as well as many other noteworthy articles on hand, but our space forbids and we think we already advanced sufficient proof of our opening assertion. The present firm is made up of Messrs. P. O'Brien and P. E. Conry, who succeeded Mr. B. Corkery in 1880. These gentlemen are both natives of Massachusetts, and are well-known in Marlboro, Mr. Conry being one of the assessors. Messrs. O'Brien & Conry give close attention to the interests of their patrons and guarantee the prompt and accurate filling of orders.

Star Furniture Co., manufacturers, wholesale and retail dealers in Furniture and Carpets, No. 103 Main Street, Lawrence Block, Marlboro, Mass.—The selection of furniture and carpets is one of the most difficult, and at the same time one of the most pleasureable duties that falls to the lot of the householder and this particular duty is rendered all the more pleasant by visiting an establishment where such a large and varied stock is carried as to suit all tastes, as well as all purses. It is just such an establishment that is carried on by the Star Furniture Co., at No. 103 Main street, Marlboro, and during the period that this company has been identified with its present line of business it has gained a high reputation for the excellence of its goods, the lowness of its prices and the uniformly fair and equitable dealing that is extended to all. The premises utilized comprise two floors, 50 × 144 feet, and 25 × 50 feet respectively in addition to a spacious store-house. The extensive stock of furniture and carpets that may be found here, is remarkable in more respects than one, but chiefly on account of its great variety and the standard excellence of the articles composing it. The Star Furniture Co., which has Mr. James H. Dee for president, Mr. C. E. Cumings as treasurer, and O. W. Temple as manager, knows well that it has a reputation to maintain and takes good care that it shall not be jeopardized by any cause within the power of its management to control. A positive guarantee is given that every article manufactured, or sold at either wholesale or retail, shall prove just as represented. Four efficient assistants are employed and all visitors to this establishment will receive prompt and courteous attention. The line of furniture and carpets shown is well made and first-class in all respects and is worthy the inspection of all desiring reliable and fashionable goods at moderate prices.

Rice & Hutchins, Cotting Ave. and Middlesex Factories, Marlboro.—It is impossible to manufacture to the best advantage many different lines in one factory, however large or well equipped it may be. Every locality has a specialty in which its mechanics have become experts. In order to produce to the greatest perfection and at the lowest cost, a complete variety of goods for men's, boys' and youths' wear, Messrs. Rice & Hutchins have established over half a dozen factories in as many different localities. The Marlboro business of this firm finally outgrowing even the frequent additions to the old buildings, it became necessary to erect the new shops, views of which are here given.

COTTING AVENUE FACTORY.

FACTORY "B," MARLBORO, MASS.

Among its productions of 2000 pairs and more per day, the Cotting avenue factory turns out the finer grades of sewed veal calf and buff, together with medium and low priced calf, buff and veal calf men's, boys' and youths' machine sewed shoes.

MIDDLESEX FACTORY.

FACTORY "A," MARLBORO, MASS.

The Middlesex factory produces about 2000 pairs per day of the more solid and substantial lines of men's, boys' and youths' veal calf and split standard screw shoes, for hard wear, in tap and half double sole.

Both factories are modern in their construction, the Cotting avenue being but a year old, and they are fully equipped with every improved machine necessary to obtain the best possible work in every part of the shoes made in them. They are

thoroughly fitted out with sprinklers, fire pails, hydrants, fire pumps and double water supply for fire protection. Over 700 expert people are employed, and over one million pairs of shoes are annually produced.

Mr. J. E. Curtis, one of the most respected and most capable manufacturers in the State, manages both shops with the aid of skilful assistants in all departments.

Messrs. Rice & Hutchins carry at their store, 125 Summer street, Boston, a complete stock of all their staple productions in order to supply the jobbing trade without the delay necessary when making goods to order.

Marlboro Savings Bank, 38 Mechanics St., Marlboro.—The Boston Sunday *Herald* recently published interviews with several of the leading business men of that city, in which they briefly sketched the methods by which they had attained their present prominence, and as all of them are strictly "self made men," their stories are of value to every young man who is beginning as they did, with no capital and no influential friends. The main principle inculcated by their business histories is the importance of saving money. Of course they all endeavored to make themselves indispensable to their employers and to gain a comprehensive knowledge of their line of business aside from mastering their own special duties; but while doing this, and while only earning from three to five dollars a week, they were steadily amassing a fund for future use. One of the largest dry goods dealers in Boston to-day—a man who can draw his check for a million in the full assurance that it will be duly honored—began business for himself less than forty years ago, his sole capital being $400 which he had saved in five years out of a salary averaging but four dollars per week. He says: "The habit of saving is as easily formed as the habit of spending; it is easier to save the second hundred than the first, and the young man who doesn't want to begin where his employer left off will find no difficulty in saving money faster than I could, for wages are much higher and the cost of living has not increased correspondingly." There is food for reflection in that statement, and perhaps some of our readers may profit by the lesson it teaches.

That many of the residents of Marlboro and vicinity do save money regularly is proved by the books of the Marlboro Savings Bank, and it is a gratifying fact that the $1,200,000 deposited in that institution is made up entirely of the savings of the people. The bank was incorporated in 1860 and has become so well and favorably known throughout this section that any explanation of its aims and any eulogy of its management would be entirely superfluous. Its financial condition is beyond criticism and the character and ability of the men having it in charge form the best of reasons for believing that the bank's future will be worthy of its past. The president is Mr. S. Herbert Howe, the treasurer, Mr. Edward R. Alley, and the board of investment is composed of Messrs. S. H. Howe, W. D. Burdett, L. S. Brigham, A. C. Weeks and Winslow M. Warren.

The bank has always been ably managed, but

upon the accession of Mr. Elbridge Howe to the presidency in the year 1876 or '7, a decided change was made in its policy and it became more a savings bank of the people than a depository of wealthy men, and when its present treasurer, Mr. Edward R. Alley, assumed the charge of its financial management, the entire board of its officers were in accord. Mr. Alley, although a young man, has been long and favorably known to the people of Marlboro and its surrounding towns, and the bank's many depositors justly believe his word to be law. Upon the death of Mr Elbridge Howe in 1886 Mr. S. Herbert Howe was chosen president, and the continued growth and prosperity of the bank fully justifies the choice. The whole secret of the success and soundness of this bank is its policy in the interest of its depositors and the individual attention given to all applications for loans by its board of investment.

The S. H. Howe Shoe Co., Marlboro, Mass.—

Notwithstanding the leading position held by Massachusetts in relation to the shoe manufacturing industry, and the many immense factories devoted to this branch of production within the limits of the State, there are few establishments of such enormous capacity as that carried on by the S. H. Howe Shoe Company, for these works are capable of turning out 10,000 pairs of shoes a day—more than enough to supply the entire standing army of the United States. So vast an enterprise as this is not built up in a day, and the undertaking in question was founded over a quarter of a century ago, Mr. S. H. Howe being the original proprietor. This gentleman is president of the present company, and has long been classed among the best known and most successful shoe manufacturers in the country. The treasurer, Mr. W. E. Dadman, is also very widely and prominently known in business circles, and the various departments of the enterprise are all in charge of experienced and able men who successfully co-operate in combining the greatest possible accuracy, uniformity and economy in the many processes incidental to manufacture. The company was incorporated in 1887, with a capital of $200,000 and operates at least as perfect and as elaborate a plant as can be found in New England. The premises utilized comprise, first, the regular factory, which measures 45×150 feet, with ell 45×65 feet. A large tower has been added to this factory, the first floor being occupied for office purposes, and the second floor being utilized as the director's room. The next in order is factory known as Diamond F, dimensions being 110×28 feet, four stories, with ell 40×95 feet, and having another wing 90×60 feet, of equal height. Factory No. 3, which is known as Diamond O, is 110×30 feet. Employment is given to 700 operatives, the capacity of the works being as before stated, 10,000 pairs per day. The company manufacture shoes of every description, including men's, boys', youths', women's, misses' and children's light and heavy, medium and cheap, and as may well be imagined, are in a position to fill the heaviest orders at comparatively short notice, as well as to quote the very lowest market rates. The goods give excellent satisfaction to consumers and the trade and the business, large as it is, has by no means reached its full development.

D. W. Cosgrove, Boots, Shoes and Rubbers, 174 Main Street, Marlboro.—The boots and shoes offered at the establishment conducted by Mr. D. W. Cosgrove, at No. 174 Main street, are claimed to be "beautiful in style, perfect in fit, reliable in wear, moderate in price," and it naturally follows that if these claims are justified by the facts, no better place can possibly be found at which to procure foot wear. Well, it is easy to ascertain the truth in the matter, for the store is certainly conveniently located and we can assure our readers that every caller is given prompt and polite attention. The premises are 25×80 feet in dimensions and the stock is correspondingly large, being complete in every department and comprising the very latest fashionable novelties together with full lines of more staple goods. This business was founded in 1871, and an idea of its present magnitude may be gained from the fact that employment is given to five assistants. So large a trade as this indicates, in a community so well supplied with shoe stores as Marlboro is, argues the offering of many genuine inducements, and we believe it to be a fact that in no similar establishment in New England, Boston not excepted, can more value be obtained for money paid. Mr. Cosgrove handles the productions of the leading manufacturers, and sells no goods that cannot be warranted to prove just as represented. Style, comfort and durability are all provided for, and the assortment of sizes is so varied as to enable the most difficult feet to be satisfactorily fitted.

F. J. Hastings & Co., dealers in Flour, Grain, Feed, Meal, Chicago Gluten Meal, Bundle Hay, etc., Faulkner Mills, Marlboro, Mass.—The only way in which an adequate idea of the immensity of the trade in flour, grain, feed, meal, etc., can be obtained, is by a careful review of the concerns located in this State alone, that devote their entire attention to handling the commodities mentioned. We find houses that were established decades ago identified with this branch of commerce, and still increasing the amount of their transactions with every added year. Prominent among the concerns engaged in this line of business in Marlboro is that of Messrs. F. J. Hastings & Co., located on Lincoln street, Carter's Block. The mills of this firm are located at South Acton, and they also have an elevator at Concord, Mass. The premises at corner of Lincoln and Mechanic streets was established about 1881, and comprises a store on the lower floor of the main building, and a large warehouse in the rear. This firm do a large wholesale and retail business, and no house in this vicinity enjoys more favorable relations with their customers, and none are better able to supply goods at bottom prices, while they strictly adhere to every agreement entered into. The goods dealt in by Messrs. F. J. Hastings & Co., include flour, grain, feed, meal, bundle hay and straw, land fertilizer, horse and cattle condition food, salt, hen feed, shells, scraps, etc., grass and field seeds, also farming tools. This firm were the first to introduce to the farmers in this vicinity the CHICAGO GLUTEN MEAL, which has gained for itself an enviable reputation as the best milk-producing feed in the market.

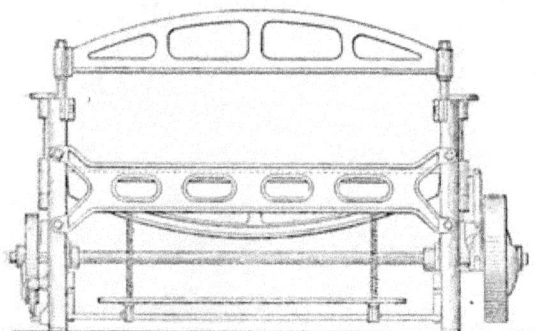

short order when circumstances render haste imperative, and it is within bounds to say that Mr. Parsons has saved local manufacturers thousands of dollars by the work he has done in this line during the past twenty years. He is prepared to furnish automatic safety elevators, the "Eclipse" sole leather cutter, rolling and stripping machines, friction treadles for sewing machines, and all kinds of boot and shoe machinery. Steam or water heating apparatus will be put into public or private buildings and guaranteed to do all that is claimed for it when properly used; and shafting and self-oiling, adjustable hangers, all sizes are carried in stock and will be put in position by competent workmen at moderate rates. Employment is given to thirty-five men, and every order is assured immediate and painstaking attention.

Henry Parsons, Machinist, and Manufacturer of Steam Engines, Marlboro, Mass.—In such an extensive manufacturing centre as Marlboro, well-equipped machine shops where repairing of all kinds can be done at short notice are a necessity, and our manufacturers have reason to congratulate themselves that the field is so well filled as is the case, for under present conditions long and costly delays from the breaking down of machinery, are rendered almost impossible. The shop carried on by Mr. Henry Parsons, occupies a leading position among such enterprises, for it has been in operation for over a score of years and has made an enviable record in the prompt and accurate filling of orders. Business was begun by Messrs. Estey & Parsons, in 1868, and the present proprietor has had sole control for about fifteen years. Mr. Parsons carries on a general machine business, and makes a specialty of the repairing of steam engines, having a force of men experienced in such work, as well as improved tools and appliances especially adapted to the purpose. A job can be "rushed through" in very

A. C. Weeks, dealer in Hardware, Crockery, Shoe Kit, Window Glass, Drain Pipe, Leather Belting, etc., 158 Main Street, Marlboro, Mass.—There are many retail establishments in Marlboro which are well and favorably known throughout that community, and there are some which enjoy quite an extensive out of town patronage also, but it would be difficult, if not impossible, to name one more highly regarded and more liberally supported by both local and suburban customers than that conducted by Mr. A. C. Weeks at No. 158 Main street. The confidence reposed in this enterprise by the general public is the legitimate result of the policy pursued for more than a score of years, for operations were begun in 1867 and from that time to the present no trouble has been spared to fully satisfy all reasonable purchasers. Mr. Weeks is a native of Warren, N. H., and has long been looked upon as one of Marlboro's representative citizens. He has held the position of town treasurer for seventeen years, and is so extensively known in this section as to render detailed personal mention quite unnecessary. Mr. Weeks deals in a great variety of articles, including hardware, crockery, shoe kit, window glass, drain pipe, agricultural tools and machinery, leather belting, etc., and carries on the largest store of the kind in this vicinity, the premises occupied comprising one floor and a basement measuring 30 × 65 feet, together with a spacious storehouse. Employment is given to four competent assistants, and customers are sure of receiving immediate and careful attention, while Mr. Week's favorable relations with producers and wholesalers, and his policy of being content with a moderate profit, combine to make it worth the while of everyone wanting anything in his line to give him a call, as the prices quoted are invariably as low as the lowest and the goods are sure to prove just precisely as represented.

John J. Skahan, Auctioneer (Sales attended in any part of the State), Office, 7 Mechanics Street, Marlboro, Mass.—The advantages gained by employing a competent auctioneer when any property is to be offered at public auction are too obvious to require detailed mention, and as circumstances may at any time render it expedient for some of our readers to hold such a sale, we take pleasure in calling attention to the facilities possessed by Mr. John J. Skahan, whose office is located at No. 7 Mechanic street, for this gentleman has had a wide and varied experience in the performance of the responsible duties of an auctioneer and has a well earned reputation for ability and devotion to the interests of those availing themselves of his services. He is prepared to attend sales in any part of the State at short notice, and has a store in Marlboro in which he carries on an auction and commission business. Mr. Skahan's terms are moderate, and the best possible proof of his ability and discretion is that afforded by the flattering endorsement of those who have profited by his services since he began operations in this town in 1887. He is a native of Hudson, Mass., and is extremely well known in business circles throughout this section. Mr. Skahan, in addition to his auction business is a real estate agent, and has on hand at all times bargains in real estate.

Frank E. Brigham, Feed, Livery, Hack and Boarding Stable. Hacks for Funerals, Parties and Weddings at Short Notice. 177 Lincoln Street (rear Marlboro Hotel), Marlboro, Mass.— Probably one of the oldest and best known livery and hack stables to be found in Marlboro is that located at 177 Lincoln street (rear of Marlboro Hotel) and now conducted by Mr. Frank E Brigham, for this stable was founded in 1868, and has been steadily carried on ever since, the present proprietor succeeding his father at his death which occurred in 1886, since which date Mr. Frank E. Brigham has striven to make the establishment a most popular one. He has constantly improved the efficiency of the service in every possible way, and has tried to furnish horses and stylish, easy-riding carriages, and has in short striven to give customers full value for money received in every case. The premises occupied are located at the above address, and every accommodation is afforded for fifteen horses and a large number of carriages, etc. A sufficient force is employed to keep everything in neat and presentable condition, and the attention of horse owners is called to the inducements here offered for the boarding and feeding of

horses. The charges for livery and hack service are very reasonable, and of themselves furnish strong inducements to patronize this establishment. Mr. Brigham is a native of Minnesota, and gives prompt attention to all orders, and hacks are furnished for funerals, parties, weddings, etc., at the shortest possible notice.

H. C. Wright, dealer in Dry Goods, etc., agent for Butterick's Patterns, and Lewando's French Dye House, 152 and 154 Main Street, Marlboro.— The establishment conducted by Mr. H. C. Wright is the largest dry goods store in town, and the stock carried will compare favorably in point of extent and variety, with that offered at many city stores making great pretensions. Mr. Wright is a native of Hyannis, Mass., and has been identified with this establishment since 1873. He has built up a reputation for enterprise and honorable dealing which is by no means confined to Marlboro, but which extends throughout this section and has resulted in the establishment of a large and growing out-of-town trade. The premises made use of are located at No. 152 Main street, and are 33 × 60 feet in dimensions, being equipped with every facility for the accommodation of customers, and the proper storage of the almost endless variety of goods comprised within the stock; embracing foreign and domestic dry and fancy goods, small wares, cloaks, shawls, gloves, hosiery, corsets, underwear and many other commodities. There are eleven assistants employed in this store, and not the least popular feature of the management is the uniformly prompt and polite attention assured to every caller. You may come here to buy or merely to look, and in either case you are sure of receiving immediate attention, and intelligent and cheerfully given information. Mr. Wright is agent for Butterick's patterns, and also for Lewando's French Dye House. He quotes bottom prices on the many articles handled, and goods can be guaranteed to prove as represented.

GEORGE F. SQUIRE,

DEALER IN

WATCHES, CLOCKS, JEWELRY, SILVERWARE,

OPTICAL GOODS, ETC.

REPAIRING A SPECIALTY.

Franklin Block. - - - *Marlboro, Mass.*

BARRY & WAUGH,

DEALERS IN

Boots, Shoes, Rubbers and Slippers,

230 MAIN STREET, MARLBORO.

All the Leading Styles in the Market kept constantly on hand.

W. H. Onthank, Hack, Livery, Boarding and Feed Stable; Hacks for Parties and Funerals, near Old Colony Depot, Florence Street, Marlboro, Mass.—The more enjoyment a man gets from driving, the more his pleasure is dependent upon having a good turnout, for one who has had but little experience on the road is generally satisfied with about any kind of a team, provided the horse be " quiet" and the carriage good and strong, while the experienced driver would rather stay at home than have to urge a lazy or old animal along. It is therefore perfectly natural that one of the first questions asked by those who are really fond of driving, should be, " where can I hire a good team?" when arriving in a town with which they are not acquainted, and the chances are that the large majority of Marlboro's residents would answer: " Go to Onthank's stable, on Florence street, near the Old Colony Depot." This business was founded about thirty years ago, so it is not surprising that it should be one of the best known enterprises of the kind in this section, especially as it has held its present leading position for many years. Mr. W. H. Onthank is a native of Southboro, and has a large circle of friends in Marlboro and adjoining towns. He has some fine turnouts for livery purposes, and although doing an extensive business can fill orders very promptly, as his facilities are of the best, and employment is given to five assistants. Hacks will be furnished for parties, funerals and other public occasions, at short notice and at moderate rates, and a large boarding and feed business is also done.

Fred A. Moore, dealer in Fine Paper Hangings, Window Shades, Room and Cornice Mouldings, etc.; Tinting and Decorating in Paper, Water or Oil Colors a Specialty. With Misses Paine & Lowe, Art Store, 139 Main Street, Marlboro, Mass.—That there is an opportunity for the display of no mean degree of taste and skill in the selection and application of wallpaper our readers will readily admit, for colors and patterns suited to certain circumstances and conditions would be strangely out of place were the surroundings different. From the very nature of the subject no unalleviating rules can be given for guidance when making such selection, although it is generally considered that small figures should be chosen for small apartments and that dark papers should not be used in rooms imperfectly lighted, but the most important rule to observe, after all, is to make your selection from a stock that is not only large and varied but that contains a full assortment of the latest patterns, for there is fashion in wall-paper as in everything else, and few of us want to be " behind the times." Mr. Fred A. Moore began business in Marlboro in 1888, and his store, located at 139 Main street, has become a popular place at which to purchase everything in the line of paper hangings, etc., for this gentleman is a retail dealer in these goods and carries a choice assortment, which he is in a position to sell at the lowest market rates, and an excellent opportunity is afforded to make an intelligent selection. Two assistants are employed, and will be found not only attentive and well-informed but also ready to lend any assistance which their experience may suggest, if so desired. Window shades, room and cornice mouldings, etc., are also dealt in and decided inducements are offered to purchasers. Mr. Moore makes a specialty of tinting and decorating in paper, and water and oil colors. He is a native of Marlboro, and is highly respected in Marlboro as an enterprising business man.

Geo. O. Levasseur, Pharmacist, Marlboro, Mass.—It is generally appreciated that "time is money," but it is apt to be forgotten that time is often more than that—being in some instances equivalent to life itself. It not infrequently happens that a serious delay in the compounding of a physician's prescription or in the obtaining of some drug or medicine, may be the means of turning the scale in favor of death in a fight against disease, and therefore it is obvious that every resident of a community is directly interested in the establishment and maintenance of drug stores, when conducted by competent parties. Those residing in Marlboro and vicinity may well congratulate themselves on the perfection of the service rendered by Mr. Levasseur, but they should not forget to encourage that gentleman to continue operations here by patronizing his establishment whenever circumstances will permit. He carries a complete assortment of drugs, medicines and chemicals, comprising everything necessary for the compounding of physicians' prescriptions in general. He is uniformly moderate in his charges and his establishment has attained a more than local reputation. Stationery, toilet articles, confectionery, cigars and tobacco, and other goods are dealt in to a considerable extent, and the employment of efficient assistants assures prompt and courteous attention to every caller, and it is natural that he should have built up a large and steadily growing patronage.

David Harris, Steam Marble and Granite Works; Monuments, Head Stones, Curbing, etc. Howe Street, Marlboro, Mass.—It is comparatively easy to decide where to place an order for something in common use, as for instance, clothing, groceries, etc., for everyone is more or less familiar with such articles, and has a comparatively accurate idea as to what they should cost and what their quality should be; but when it comes to placing orders for monumental work or stone work of any kind, some little difficulty is met with, and therefore a word or two relative to the facilities possessed by Mr. David Harris, will doubtless be appreciated by such of our readers as contemplate the purchase of anything in this line, for Mr. Harris carries on excellently equipped steam marble and granite works, and is prepared to do either monumental or ornamental stone cutting at short notice, and in a superior manner. He was born in England and has conducted his present establishment since 1882. It is located on Howe street, and those interested in cemetery work will find it well worthy of a visit, for many tasteful designs are shown, and the workmanship is equal to the best in every respect. Monuments, headstones, tablets, mantel pieces, vases, urns, curbing—in short, marble and granite work of all descriptions is done at moderate rates, and the employment of eight experienced assistants enables commissions to be promptly executed. Estimates will be cheerfully made and all desired information given.

HISTORICAL SKETCH

OF

HUDSON.

Hudson is one of the frontier towns of Middlesex County, being located in its northwest part, adjoining the county of Worcester. The town is bounded on the north by Bolton and Stow, on the south by Marlborough, on the west by Berlin and on the east by Sudbury. Its surface is comparatively level although by no means flat, most of it being composed of gently undulating land, although in the northwest corner it is bold and rugged, while there is one very considerable hill—Mount Assabet—on the south side of the river opposite the village. This eminence reaches a height of about 150 feet and is very gracefully proportioned, being free from abrupt outlines and most admirably adapted to use as a site for the beautiful residences now becoming so common throughout the State. Many other eligible sites are available within the limits of the town and it is safe to say there is not a community in this section of the State offering more genuine inducements to those seeking a healthful, sightly and convenient location for a country residence. The railroad facilities are good and as Boston is but twenty-eight miles distant, all the important trade centers are easily accessible from the village. Hudson makes a very favorable showing as an agricultural community, although chiefly known in connection with her manufacturing interests, for her soil is productive and may be tilled with comparative ease and the resident farmers are men of ability and enterprise.

The early history of Hudson is of course merged into that of the towns from which it was formed, for although Hudson has not yet finished the first quarter century of her corporate existence, the territory comprised within her limits has been settled for more than two hundred years and its history forms a part of the records of Marlborough, of Sudbury, of Bolton and of Lancaster. It would be quite impossible within our limited space to give even a summary of the many events of which accounts are preserved in these records, but our readers will find some of the more important of them spoken of in the historical sketches of Marlborough and adjoining towns contained in this volume. In many instances the most careful research will fail to give credit where credit is due in apportioning the part which the residents

WOOD'S SQUARE HUDSON.

of the future Hudson took in the development of the community, for historians seldom specify very nicely in their accounts and it is thought sufficient to record that a certain act was performed by the citizens of a certain town, without regard to whether they resided in the northern or the southern portion of it. That part of Marlborough which was finally set apart to form Hudson was not settled so speedily as the other portions of the town for a number of reasons, the most important of which was that no valid title to the land could be given, owing to complications arising from Indian grants. Settlers, of course, did not care to have the labor of years in such jeopardy as the cultivation of land which could not be legally sold or transferred would necessarily entail, and until 1719, when this drawback was removed, very little progress was made. A grist-mill was built in 1700, on the Assabet River, the site belonging to Joseph Howe, whose daughter married Jeremiah Barstow, who thus became the owner of the property, which he sold in 1723 to Robert Barnard, of Andover, Barnard coming to town the following year and opening a public house besides operating the mill. Other settlers gradually came in, among them being Solomon Brigham, grandfather of Charles and Francis Brigham, who have done much to make Hudson what it now is. Joel Cranston came to the village from the eastern part of the town in 1794 and opened a store and a tavern.

He was a pushing, progressive man and induced some valuable citizens to take up their residence in the village, among them being George Peters, a blacksmith; Jedediah Wood, a wool carder; Stephen Pope, a tanner; Folger Pope, a harness maker; and Ebenezer Witt, a miller.

Cranston formed a partnership with Silas Felton, and these two men greatly advanced the interests of the village, which was known as "Feltonville," when Hudson was incorporated. At a meeting held May 3, 1865, steps were taken to

TOWN HALL, HUDSON, MASS.

bring about a separation, and May 19, 1866, the Legislature passed the act of incorporation but did not include that part of the territory desired, lying within the town of Bolton. Rather than have any hard feelings in the matter, the residents of Hudson and of that portion of Bolton which desired to be set off, left the question in dispute to arbitration, and it was amicably settled by the payment to Bolton of $10,000 and the acquisition of the desired tract. The new town was named in honor of Charles Hudson of Lexington, and to show his appreciation of the compliment, he offered to give $500 towards the establishment of a free town library, provided the townspeople would appropriate a similar sum. The offer was accepted and the library opened in 1867, since which date it has been liberally supported and has fully justified the hopes of its founders. At the first town meeting $3000 was appropriated for schools, and from that day to this the cause of education has been aided by liberal supplies of money and by careful and skillful supervision. Religious instruction has also been provided from the very first, and the several

religious societies of the town are in a very flourishing condition. After schools,
roads, etc., were given proper attention, the town decided that a public hall was a
pressing necessity, and the result was the erection of a handsome, commodious and
substantial building at a total cost—site, building and furnishing included—of
$58,500. It is most conveniently arranged and is a credit to all who had a hand in
its design and construction.

HUDSON, MASS., HIGH SCHOOL.

Shoe manufacturing may be said to have been begun in Hudson in 1815, for in
that year a modest business was established by one who employed three assistants
and made "sale" shoes. The real origin of the industry, however, was in 1835,
when Francis Brigham inaugurated those operations which were destined to have so
important a bearing on the town's future. He began on a small scale, but rapidly
extended his business and attracted such favorable attention to Hudson that it has
become one of the most famous shoe manufacturing towns in the State. Many
tributary branches of manufacture are carried on here as well as some independent
industries and there seems to be no reasonable doubt that Hudson has entered upon
a career of permanent prosperity. The advantages she offers are solid and genuine;
her railroad and banking facilities are first-class, the society is cultured and agreeable, and take it all in all, Hudson fully merits her high reputation as a manufacturing and commercial centre and as a pleasant and healthful place of residence.

LEADING BUSINESS MEN

HUDSON, MASS.

P. E. Millay & Son, manufacturers of all kinds of Boot and Shoe Lasts. Contracts taken for Lasts, Dies and Patterns. Sole Patterns a specialty. Hudson, Mass.—The enterprise carried on by Messrs. P. E. Millay & Son was inaugurated just thirty years ago by Mr. P. E. Millay, and though the demand for the goods produced has reached great magnitude at the present time, the firm were never better prepared to fill the most extensive orders at the shortest possible notice. Mr. P. E. Millay is a native of Whitefield, Maine, while Mr. F. W. Millay was born in South Danvers, Mass., and became a member of the firm in 1886. The premises utilized for manufacturing purposes comprise two floors of the dimensions of 30 × 60 feet, and two spacious store houses are also made use of, as the firm carry a heavy and varied stock which is constantly being renewed and which enables many orders to be filled without the least delay. The factory is fitted up with improved machinery and employment is given to nine skilled assistants in the manufacture of boot and shoe lasts of all kinds, dies, patterns, etc.; a specialty is made of sole patterns, and goods are sold directly to manufacturers, contracts being taken for lasts, dies and patterns, and agreements being carried out to the letter. The distinguishing features of the policy pursued by this firm are "good work," "promptness," "best styles" and "fair prices," and this being the case it is not surprising that the business should be in a most prosperous condition. All orders are assured immediate and careful attention, and no inferior work is allowed to leave the factory.

Andrew Blyth, manufacturer of Home-made and Cream Bread, all kinds of Plain and Fancy Cake. Sale store, Jefts' Block, Main Street; Bakery, Broad Street, Hudson, Mass.—That some persons are prejudiced against "bakers' bread" is undeniable, and it is no wonder that such should be the case, for the goods offered by some bakers are certainly not all that they should be and are really unfit for domestic use. But it is poor policy to condemn all on account of the transgressions of a few, and it is undeniable that the bread, cake and pastry sold at certain public bakeries will compare very favorably with the choicest "home-made" productions. Of such quality are the goods handled by Mr. Andrew Blyth, and that his productions are acceptable to the most fastidious is proved by the character as well as by the magnitude of his trade. He is a native of Scotland and has carried on operations in this town since 1884. The bakery is fitted up with the most improved appliances and is located on Broad street, the sale store being in Jefts' block, Main street. Mr. Blyth does both a wholesale and retail business, dealing in home-made and cream bread, plain and fancy cake of every description, and all the goods usually kept in a first-class bakery. Wedding cakes will be made to order at short notice, and picnic and other pleasure parties will be supplied with substantials and delicacies at very reasonable prices. Mr. Blyth gives careful personal attention to his business and spares no pains to fully satisfy every customer.

L. T. Jefts, manufacturer of Women's, Misses' and Children's Kip and Imitation Kip, Veal Calf and Imitation Goat, Pegged and Standard Screw, Polka and Polish Boots and Balmorals, with Raw Hide, Metallic, Box and Union Tips; also Joyce's Patent Protection Toe. Manufactory at Hudson, Mass. Salesroom at 103 Summer and 92 Bedford Streets, Boston.—Mr. L. T. Jefts is one of the most prominent manufacturers doing business in this section of the State, having been located in Hudson for over thirty years, and his factory is one of the most perfectly equipped establishments of the kind to be found in New England, both as regards the character and extent of the machinery it contains, and the provision which has been made to avoid serious loss by fire, for the manufacturing plant is made up of the most improved and efficient labor-saving machinery, which is run by a forty horse engine, and the premises are thoroughly fitted up with automatic sprinklers and an electric fire alarm. The main factory is four stories in height and 113 × 30 feet in dimensions, and there is a four-story wing attached, measuring 25 × 37 feet. Employment is given to 140 assistants who produce some 2000 pairs of boots and balmorals daily. Mr. Jefts manufactures women's, misses' and children's buff, kip and imitation kip, veal calf and imitation goat, pegged and standard screw polka and polish boots and balmorals, with raw hide, metallic, box and Union tips. His goods are too well known to the trade to require detailed mention, and have for years been accepted as the standard from which to judge articles of similar grade. They are exceptionally durable, and combine strength and comfort to an uncommon degree. A salesroom is maintained at No. 103 Summer and No. 92 Bedford streets, Boston, and the facilities are such as to enable the largest orders to be filled at short notice. Correspondence may be addressed to Hudson or Boston, and will receive immediate and careful attention. Mr. Jefts is a native of Washington, N. H. (to which town he donated a fine public library in 1879), and as previously stated began operations in Hudson more than thirty years ago. In 1868 the firm of Jefts & Smith was formed, Mr. Jefts again becoming sole proprietor in 1869. In 1870 Messrs. Jefts & Davis continued the enterprise, and in 1872 Mr. Jefts resumed entire control, which he has since retained. He has served as overseer of the poor, and on the school committee, and has occupied the position of president of the Hudson National Bank since that institution was founded. Mr. Jefts served in the house of representatives in 1883. He was also a member of the senate during the years 1886 and 1887, since which time he has been a member of the State central committee.

Levi P. Ellithorp, Cloth and Velvet Covered Caskets of every description; also Coffins and Ladies' and Gents' Robes, Wreaths, Crosses and Cut Flowers Furnished. Main Street, Hudson, Mass.—There is at least as great an opportunity for the display of taste in the choosing of caskets, coffins and other funeral goods, as in the selection of any other commodities, and Mr. Levi P. Ellithorp renders a general service to the public by offering an exceptionally large assortment of such articles, as his stock is sufficiently varied to admit of all tastes and circumstances being suited. He deals in coffins, and in cloth and velvet covered caskets of every description, as well as in funeral robes of all kinds, and the prices quoted are in no case exorbitant, being as low as are named anywhere on goods of equal grade. Another department of his business, and one that has proved of decided convenience to the public, is that devoted to the furnishing of floral emblems of every approved design, comprising wreaths, crosses, columns and other articles, cut flowers in general also being supplied in any desired quantity. Mr. Ellithorp is in a position to fill all orders at very short notice, and the facilities at his command are very generally availed of by the residents of Hudson and vicinity.

A. M. Pitt, Florist, Conservatories on High Street, Hudson, Mass.—The language of flowers comes the nearest to that "universal language" which so many have attempted to establish, of any with which we are familiar, for sorrow, joy, sympathy and congratulation can all be expressed in this tongue in a manner no one can fail to understand. A floral emblem will often convey sentiments which it would be difficult to express so satisfactorily in any other way, and it is but natural that the demand for flowers and for emblematic designs should increase as civilization advances. Some idea of what this increase has been may be gained by comparing the facilities now employed by a leading florist of Hudson, A. M. Pitt, who succeeded Mr. Geo. Houghton in 1889. Mr. Houghton carried on operations over fifteen years. At that time the demand for flowers was small compared with the present. The premises occupied are located at the corner of High and Main streets, Hudson, and consist of four greenhouses, one of which measures 20×60 feet, two 12×50 feet, and one 12×47 feet in dimensions. These greenhouses are equipped with the latest improved apparatus, and both a wholesale and retail business is extensively and successfully conducted. Prompt and careful attention is given to all orders whether by mail or otherwise, and a strict personal oversight in all matters pertaining to this business, has resulted in securing the confidence and patronage of so large a number of the residents of this town and vicinity.

James Burkill, Merchant Tailor, Hudson, Mass.—Shakespeare says, "Rich be thy apparel as thy purse can buy" and like many another of his sayings, this bit of advice is as valuable at the present time as at the date when it was written. The well dressed man enjoys more consideration in this world than he who contents himself with shabby attire, and the young man in business life who wants to make a favorable impression, cannot be too careful to dress fashionably and neatly. Of course, one's purchases should be guided by good taste, and "extreme" styles should be avoided, but make it a point to wear good fitting and well-made garments and you will find the money they cost is well invested. We know of no better place to obtain fashionable clothing at a moderate cost, than at the establishment conducted by Mr. James Burkill, for this gentleman is a merchant tailor of long experience, and offers his customers many genuine advantages. He is a native of England, served in the army for two years, and began operations in this town in 1876. An entire building, two and one-half stories in height and 20 × 40 feet in dimensions, is occupied, and an exceptionally large and varied stock of woolens is shown, comprising the latest patterns in foreign and domestic fabrics, and also a full line of staple goods. Mr. Burkill allows no inferior work to leave his store, and guarantees satisfaction to his customers. Honest goods, careful and thorough workmanship, perfection of fit and uniformly reasonable prices make a very attractive combination, so that it is natural that this establishment should be extremely popular among those conversant with the methods that characterize its management. Employment is given to five competent assistants, and orders are assured immediate attention.

Tower Brothers, Boot and Shoe Machinery. Special attention given to fitting up Manufactories, Hudson, Mass.—Even the most improved and efficient machinery will not of course assure success in shoe manufacturing, any more than it will in any other branch of industry, for business ability and enterprise are indispensable in these days of close competition, but it is not to be disputed that, other things being equal, the most perfectly equipped factory can turn out the best work at the lowest prices, and this being the case, the importance of using care in the selection and maintenance of a mechanical plant becomes obvious. The firm of Tower Brothers, doing business on Loring street, handle boot and shoe machinery of all descriptions and make a specialty of shafting hangers and pulleys, and steam fitting, and give special attention to the fitting up of manufactories. The undertaking carried on by them was founded by Mr. F. A. Davidson in 1858, he being succeeded by the present firm in 1868, so that Messrs. Tower Brothers have about twenty-one years of experience to guide them in carrying on operations to the best advantage. During this period they have equipped a number of large establishments besides filling many smaller commissions, and the record made thus far furnishes the best possible proof of their ability to fill orders to the satisfaction of all parties concerned. The firm is made up of Messrs. H. C., and J. N. Tower, both of whom are natives of Stowe, Mass. Mr. H. C. Tower served in the army during the Rebellion, and has filled various town offices, such as selectman, assessor and water commissioner, and is also a member of the Legislature. The premises utilized have an area of 3,300 square feet and are very completely fitted up, the machinery in use being driven by a twenty-horse engine, and employment given to twelve competent assistants. Among the more important machines manufactured, may be mentioned rolling mills, moulding machines, heel filing machines, sand papering machines, heel pricking machines, heel presses, embossing machines and peg cutting machines; all of which are thoroughly well made from selected material and are guaranteed to prove equal to representations. The firm are prepared to fill orders at short notice, and at the lowest rates consistent with honest and skillful work.

A. M. Mossman, Jeweler, Watches, Clocks and Silverware, Manson's Block, Hudson, Mass. —Among the best known and most reliable establishments of this kind in Hudson is that of Mr. A. M. Mossman, which is located in Manson's Block. Mr. Mossman has a well-earned reputation for the excellence of his wares, and the fidelity with which work entrusted is performed hence his business is prosperous and steadily increasing. With the advancement of any community in wealth, intelligence and culture, the fine arts of decoration and adornment prosper, and the skill and taste of the watchmaker and jeweler are brought more constantly and generally into requisition. Twenty years ago it would have been impossible to have found customers for that class of goods, which now are really in the greatest demand. This store was started in 1868, by S. M. Hewitt, who was succeeded in 1878 by the present proprietor. The premises occupied comprise a store 25×50 feet in dimensions, which is very attractive in its appointments. The stock carried is very select, comprising the finest grade of watches, and a beautiful and unique selection of silverware and jewelry, calculated to please the most fastidious. Mr. Mossman is a native of Searsport, Maine, and is an experienced and practical business man. We bespeak for him a continuance of the success he has already achieved, as he is a gentleman of judgment and sound business principles, and displays taste in the selection of his stock, which embraces, in addition, all the novelties of the day in this line.

H. M. Campbell, Harness Maker, Jobbing and Repairing a Specialty. Whips, Collars, Surcingles, Brushes, Curry Combs, Halters and Harness Oils. Harnesses washed and Oiled to order. Felton Street, Hudson, Mass.—The man who said that "harnesses are of two kinds, good and bad, and most of those in the market are the latter," no doubt exaggerated the matter somewhat, but nevertheless it is undeniable that too many inferior harnesses are now made and sold. It is always worth while to get a good harness for there is no necessity for paying a fancy price for such an article, and owing to its greater strength of material and workmanship it is the most durable and the cheapest in the long run. Mr. H. M. Campbell, doing business on Felton street, manufactures and sells harnesses of every description, and those who deal with him are sure of getting full value for every dollar they pay him, as his prices are uniformly reasonable and his goods are guaranteed to prove as represented. Mr. Campbell was born in Naragaugus, Maine. He enlisted in the army at the breaking out of the war, at the age of seventeen, in the Twenty eighth Regiment Maine Volunteers, under Col. Woodbury. He opened his store in Hudson in 1887, and has built up an extensive business, which is steadily increasing, as the merits of his goods and the lowness of his prices become more generally understood. A large stock of safe harnesses is constantly on hand, together with whips, collars, surcingles, brushes, curry combs, halters and harness oils. Harnesses are washed and oiled to order, and a specialty is made of jobbing and repairing, the work being faithfully and skillfully done in every detail and orders being filled at short notice.

F. Brigham & Co., manufacturers of Women's, Misses', Children's, Men's, Boy's and Youth's Pegged and Standard Screw Shoes, No. 5 High Street, Boston, Factory at Hudson, Mass.—The business carried on under the firm name of F. Brigham & Co., was established fifty-five years ago, and has long ranked among the leading enterprises of the kind in this section of the State, it having steadily increased in magnitude until the present factory, large and well-equipped as it is, has become too small to suit the purposes of the firm, who contemplate building another factory in the immediate future. As now constituted, the concern is made up of Messrs. Rufus H., W. F., and W. H. Brigham, all of whom were born in Hudson. The premises occupied, comprise three floors, of the dimensions of 30 × 120 feet each, and are fitted up with a very extensive plant of improved machinery, which is driven by water power. Employment is given to 175 operatives who turn out some 1500 pairs of shoes per day, comprising women's, misses', children's, men's, boys' and youth's pegged and standard screw shoes, Dunham nailed shoes and sewed shoes. It will be seen that the firm manufacture a great variety of goods adapted to all ages and all conditions of wear. Messrs. F. Brigham & Co.'s productions hold a high place in the market, for dealers and consumers have learned that they are honestly made from carefully chosen material and will prove as represented in every instance. Indeed, their popularity is well indicated by the present productive capacity of 1800 pairs daily being insufficient, and there is no question but what with increased facilities, the firm will materially add to the magnitude of their business. An office and warerooms are maintained at No. 5 High street, Boston, where full lines of the various styles manufactured are kept in stock, enabling orders to be filled at short notice.

Lawrence & Wilkins, dealers in all kinds of Coal and Wood, 15 Broad Street, Hudson Mass.—Among the most important commodities of the present day there is nothing of more, or so much importance as the fuel which is used in all occupations and in all domestic departments of our homes whether they are humble or of pretentious proportions. If we were able to announce the quantity consumed even in our one State of Massachusetts, it would surprise even those most familiar with such matters, while the quantity consumed is so enormous, it is for the interest of all consumers to become familiar with the different qualities of coal and wood, and to select for their use such as will be the most economical in the end for the purpose for which it is required. As it would be impossible for all manufacturers, as well as all housekeepers to devote much time to this subject we are all inclined to trust to the coal dealer, and when we find the coal and wood to be what we require, and the price to agree with the market prices quoted, we can but feel that we are dealing with an honest man. We would call the attention of the readers of this book to the business conducted by Messrs. Lawrence & Wilkins, on Broad street. The patronage which they have received is proof that they are honorable in their dealings, and the residents of this town can testify to the promptness with which all orders are attended to.

Rufus Stratton, dealer in Meats and Vegetables of all Kinds, Wood Square, Hudson, Mass.—While speaking of the most prominent and well known business houses of Hudson we would call particular attention to that conducted by Mr. Stratton, dealer in meats and vegetables of all kinds. This establishment is the oldest of the kind in town, having been started over thirty-seven years ago. Mr. Stratton had a partner for a short time, since then he has conducted the business alone, and his successful career is a testimony of his abilities. The premises will measure 1000 square feet, and are located on Wood square, Hudson. Employment is given to two efficient and courteous assistants. Here may be found a good assortment of tea, coffee, flour and spices, canned goods, patent medicines, fruits of all kinds in their season, cigars and tobacco, as well as meats and vegetables. There is no finer assortment offered to choose from at any retail establishment in Hudson. The most fastidious can find goods precisely suited to their needs, while on the other hand no one need stay away for fear of high prices, as the rates quoted are as low as the condition of the market will permit. Orders are given prompt attention and delivered with accuracy and dispatch. Mr. Stratton is the son of Lorenzo Stratton, who was the first manufacturer of shoes in this town, having started that business in 1827. Hudson at that time was called Feltonville, and only eleven houses standing at the time the father of Rufus came to the town. Rufus Stratton is a native of Hudson, and is well known both in business and social connections. He was assessor for over three years. His years' of experience and extended reputation are sufficient to warrant the confidence of any who may wish to patronize this store for the purchase of anything which he may offer to the public.

H. Robinson, dealer in Produce and Provisions, also Fish and Oysters, Main Street, Hudson.—The establishment carried on by Mr. H. Robinson, Main street, is very popular in this section of the town, and when the stock on hand is examined and the prices learned, the reasons for this popularity become evident at once, even without taking into consideration the prompt and polite service accorded to every customer, thus accounting for the enviable reputation which has been gained. This enterprise was started in 1881 by the present proprietor, who is a native of Concord, Mass. The premises occupied will cover 800 square feet, and Mr. Robinson has also a slaughter house on River street where about all the butchering for the town is done, probably killing over 400 hogs per year. The assortment of goods on hand is extremely varied but very carefully selected, being obtained from strictly reliable sources and therefore especially suited for family trade. It comprises meats, provisions and country produce in general, and at the proper seasons, and also includes fish and oysters, which for quality and freshness cannot be excelled in town. Employment is given to two competent assistants, and as we have previously intimated, customers are waited upon promptly and politely. Quality for quality, the prices quoted are as low as the lowest, and the stock is so constituted that all tastes and all means can be catered to satisfactorily.

Whittemore & Ewell (successors to G. W. Davis), wholesale and retail dealers in Flour, Grain, Feed, Hay, Straw, etc., Poultry supplies a Specialty, Main Street, Hudson, Mass.—From its paramount importance and the character of the firms engaged in it, the wholesale trade in flour, grain, feed, hay, etc., is naturally one of the first to challenge the attention when compiling an industrial history of any section, and one of the foremost houses in this line in Hudson or vicinity is that conducted by Whittemore & Ewell on Main street. They are successors to G. W. Davis, a well-known gentleman, who started some years since in this business. In 1887 the present firm assumed the full management of affairs and they now do an extensive and increasing business, both wholesale as well as retail in flour, grain, feed, hay, straw, etc. The premises occupied in the prosecution of this business, will measure about 2500 square feet besides storeroom, which is required for the reception and storage of goods. Mr. E. Whittemore is a native of Fitzwilliam, N. H., and Mr. C. Ewell is a native of Maine. Both gentlemen are well known in this town, and the many who have enjoyed business relations with this house in the past, are aware that one of its strongest claims to patronage is the celerity and accuracy with which all orders are filled. They make a specialty of poultry supplies, and no concern is better prepared to obtain goods at the lowest rates, and all advantages held are fully shared with customers. They prepare and sell at wholesale and retail the celebrated "Peels Compound Condition Food," for horses and cattle and poultry. Their trade in this food is very large and constantly increasing. By a continuance of the strict personal oversight and attention shown in the past, the success of this house is certain.

R. A. Guernsey, dealer in All Kinds of Wood and Coal; Office in the rear of Houghton's Factory, Hudson, Mass.—Among the many enterprises conducted in this town which we wish to call especial attention to, is that carried on by R. A. Guernsey, dealer in wood and coal. This business was first started in 1877 by H Whitcomb & Co., and was well known by the residents of this vicinity, but after a period of ten years they were succeeded by Mr. R. A. Guernsey, who is a native of Pittsfield, Vt. Since 1887 Mr. Guernsey has carried on an extensive business, both wholesale and retail, in all kinds of wood and in all kinds of hard and soft coal His office is in the rear of Houghton's Factory, and he has the capacity for storing 3000 tons of coal. His terms are cash. This house should be classed among the most reliable establishments of its kind in this vicinity. Patrons and purchasers may feel assured of receiving excellent goods, honorable treatment and polite attention, while the prices are always reasonable. The trade from the start has annually grown, and the sales now reach a very handsome amount in the course of a year. Employment is given to two capable and energetic assistants, and the entire business is managed in a most able and satisfactory manner. All orders for coal or wood are attended to with care and promptness, as this house is able to compete with any in this line of business.

C. W. Holden, Dry Goods, Groceries, Crockery, Paints, Oils and Varnishes, Wood Square, Hudson, Mass.—It is about twenty-eight years since the firm of W. P. Holden & Son began operations in Hudson, and the enterprise has been under the sole control of Mr. C. W. Holden since 1886. He is a native of Waterville, Maine, and is so generally known in Hudson and vicinity that extended personal mention is quite unnecessary. Mr. Holden occupies premises of the dimensions of 33×55 feet, located in Wood Square, and containing an exceptionally extensive and varied stock made up of groceries, crockery and glass-ware, dry goods, paints, oils and varnishes and other commodities. In the confined space which is at our command, it is manifestly impossible to describe such an assortment in detail, but it is very generally understood in this vicinity that Mr. Holden handles no articles that he cannot guarantee will prove as represented, and it is also well known that no lower prices are quoted anywhere in this section on equally dependable goods. Employment is given to two competent assistants, and callers are assured prompt and courteous attention, goods being cheerfully shown and uniform politeness being the rule towards all.

F. S. Dawes, manufacturer of Cutting Dies and Chisels for Leather, Cloth, Paper, Sheet Metal, etc., corner Main and Houghton Streets, Hudson, Mass.—Cutting dies and chisels play a very important part in the manufacture of boots and shoes and other leather goods, as well as in the making of articles from cloth, paper, sheet metal and other substances, and it is of course obvious that the value of the finished product depends in a great measure on the accuracy and ease with which these dies, etc., do their work. Mr. F. S. Dawes has made a specialty of manufacturing cutting dies and chisels for nearly a quarter of a century, for he began operations here in 1866, his predecessor having been Mr. J. Monroe. Mr. Dawes is a native of Maine, and saw four years' service in the army during the Rebellion. His factory is located at the corner of Main and Houghton streets, and has an area of 2400 square feet, employment being given to eight assistants. All work done is of the best quality, new dies being warranted for thirty days, and no pains being spared to maintain the unsurpassed reputation for durability and efficiency so long held by Mr. Dawes' productions, which are widely used by manufacturers of boots and shoes, envelopes, paper collars, cuffs, boxes, rubber goods, harness, blankets, straps, toys, labels, tags and numerous other articles. All kinds of boot and shoe machinery will be furnished at the lowest market rates, and raw hide mallets are also dealt in to a considerable extent. A Boston office is maintained at No. 61 Lincoln street, and orders can be filled at very short notice.

Messrs. James T. & Ralph E. Joslin, Attorneys at Law, Hudson.—Mr. James T. Joslin is a native of Leominster, Mass., and is extremely well known in Hudson and vicinity, having maintained an office here for more than a quarter of a century. The firm also has an office in room 13, Advertiser Building, Boston, where Mr. James T. Joslin may be found Tuesdays and Fridays from 11 to 12. Mr. J. T. Joslin is a notary public. These gentlemen are insurance agents, and our Hudson readers certainly need not be told what their reputation is as regards ability and zealous devotion to the interests of their clients. We propose to speak especially of the services they are prepared to render in the placing of insurance, as they represent various leading companies and are in a position to write policies at as low rates as can be named in connection with thoroughly dependable insurance. Among these companies are the following:

Middlesex Mutual Fire Insurance Co., Concord; Fitchburg Mutual Fire Insurance Co., Fitchburg; Abington Mutual Fire Insurance Co., Abington; Cambridge Mutual Fire Insurance Co., Cambridge; Traders' and Mechanics' Mutual Fire Insurance Co., Lowell; People's Fire Insurance Co., Manchester, N. H.

As our readers will see, there is no company in this list but what has the full confidence of the public, and those who wish to obtain a maximum of security at a minimum of cost, can do no better than to give these gentlemen a call. The Hudson office is located in Jeft's Block, Main street, and callers are assured immediate and courteous attention, any desired information being cheerfully given by R. E. Joslin, who has charge of and can always be found at the Hudson office.

———

Boston Branch Boot and Shoe Store, L. V. Randall, Agent, Lewis' Block, opposite Town Hall, Hudson, Mass.—Boston being a great trade centre where the prices of all the commodities in common use are reduced to the lowest terms by active competition, it is natural that an establishment having the name of the "Boston Branch Boot and Shoe Store," should be expected to offer special inducements to customers, and we are sure that those who visit the store in question with such an expectation in mind, will not be disappointed in the advantages there presented. The premises utilized, are located in Lewis' Block, opposite the town hall, and measure 25 × 34 feet, this space being used to excellent advantage for the accommodation of an exceptionally large and well chosen stock made up of boots, shoes, rubbers and slippers of every description. It makes no difference whether you be young or old, stout or thin, rich or poor, you can find foot wear here suited to your needs in this respect, and can feel sure that you are buying at "bed rock" figures and that the goods will prove just as represented. This enterprise was started in 1885, and is very popular with all classes of buyers in Hudson and vicinity. Mr. L. V. Randall has charge of affairs, and with the aid of two assistants makes it a point to see that immediate and polite attention is given to every caller. The latest novelties in foot-wear are always to be found here, and goods are cheerfully shown on application.

Geo. B. Cochran, M. D., Druggist, Wood Square, Hudson, Mass.—It is very natural that particular confidence should be placed in a druggist who is also a physician, for although we are happy to say that the large majority of our Massachusetts pharmacists are educated, competent and reliable men, still there is a prevailing impression that he who fills such a responsible and exacting position as that held by a dispenser of drugs and medicines to the general public, cannot know too much concerning the properties and effects of the agents he handles. Consequently the popularity of the establishment conducted by George B. Cochran, M. D., in Wood square, is not to be wondered at in the least, especially as this gentleman has carried it on for nearly a score of years during which he has made a record which fully explains the cordial relations enjoyed with customers. Dr. Cochran is a native of Northfield, Vt., and is of course very widely known in Hudson and vicinity. He was formerly connected with the school committee, and is ever ready to aid in advancing the best interests of the community by all practicable means. The premises utilized by him, comprise one floor and a basement, of the dimensions of 25 × 40 feet, and contain a very large and varied stock, made up of drugs, medicines and chemicals, toilet articles, pocket cutlery, stationery, confectionery, cigars and tobacco and a full line of school supplies. The compounding of physician's prescriptions is given the most careful personal attention, and we need hardly say that no trouble is spared to avoid the least possible error, while the charges made are as low as is consistent with the use of the best obtainable ingredients. Employment is given to two assistants, and prompt and polite attention is assured to every customer, moderate prices being quoted in every department.

———

C. L. Woodbury, dealer in Fine Groceries, Provisions, Fruit, Confectionery, etc., 1 and 5 Main Street, Hudson, Mass.—The establishment carried on by Mr. C. L. Woodbury, at Nos. 1 and 5 Main street, was formerly a coöperative store, but passed into the possession of the present proprietor about fifteen years ago. Mr. Woodbury is a native of Bolton, Mass., and served a year in the army during the Rebellion. He has made his store one of the most popular of the kind to be found in this section, and its patronage is still steadily increasing. The reasons for this state of affairs are by no means hard to find, for in every intelligent community enterprise and fair dealing are sure to be appreciated and rewarded, and the residents of Hudson form no exception to the rule. The premises utilized by Mr. Woodbury have a front of 70 feet and a depth of 40 feet, giving ample room for the carrying of a large and varied stock, made up of choice staple and fancy groceries, meats and provisions in general, fruit, confectionery, cigars and tobacco, etc. These articles are all selected with a special view to the requirements of family trade, and are sure to give satisfaction, they being guaranteed to prove just as represented No exorbitant prices are quoted, the lowest market rates being adhered to, and the employment of five competent assistants assures immediate and polite attention to every customer, and the prompt and accurate delivery of orders.

Chase & Day, dealers in Meat, Vegetables, Provisions, Fine Groceries, Fruit, Chase Block, Wood Square, Hudson, Mass.—There are about as many theories as to the best way of doing business, as there are people interested enough in the subject to talk about it, but after all no improvement has been made on the good old fashioned plan of giving every customer a fair equivalent for his money, and treating him in a manner that renders it not only profitable, but pleasant to come again. Such has been the methods pursued by the firm of Chase & Day of Chase Block, Wood square, Hudson. This business was formerly conducted by H. W. Chase, who is a native of Holden, Mass.,—and who was succeeded in 1883 by the present proprietors. The premises occupied consist of one floor and basement, each 25 ×50 feet and a store house. Mr. G. L. Day is a native of Roxbury, Mass. Both gentlemen are well known in Hudson. The success of this firm has been pronounced and prominent enough to fully justify the pride they feel in their business. Provisions, meat and vegetables, fine groceries, fruits of all kinds in their season, also select flavors of the choicest fruits and spices. Their delicious purity, unequalled strength and economy, commend them to all lovers of choice flavors. These goods will all be found to be of first-class quality, and are offered to customers at but a small margin above wholesale rates. Three experienced assistants are employed, and all who visit this establishment are warranted polite and prompt service.

Hudson House, A. E. Cole, Proprietor. First-class Table; Terms Reasonable. Main Street, Hudson, Mass.—Commercial travellers have a fashion of rating cities and towns by the character of their hotel accommodations, and it would disagreeably surprise not a few communities which think very well of themselves could they see themselves as others see them, from a traveller's standpoint. In the case of Hudson, however, the surprise, if any were felt, would be of a pleasant character, for the Hudson House ranks second to no hotel of similar pretensions in New England, and those who appreciate how the best interests of a manufacturing and commercial community may be advanced by the existence of a first class and well-managed public house in its midst, need not be told that the hotel in question deserves the hearty endorsement and support of all interested in Hudson's prosperity. It was formerly owned by Mrs. F. Sawyer, but in 1885, passed under the control of its present popular proprietor, Mr. A. E. Cole. This gentleman was born in Schoharie, N. Y., and we may confidently assert without fear of successful contradiction that he "knows how to keep a hotel," in the best sense of the phrase. Mr. Cole has a commodious, pleasant and conveniently located house at his disposal, and he spares no pains to make it a genuine home for guests, and to so lodge, feed and serve his patrons that they shall have no reasonable cause for complaint. The hotel is handsomely furnished throughout, has a bath room, a barber shop and a livery and feed stable connected and is kept in the best of condition from roof to cellar, there being nine competent assistants employed, and every detail of the work carefully supervised. Accommodations can be provided for sixty guests, and the terms are remarkably moderate.

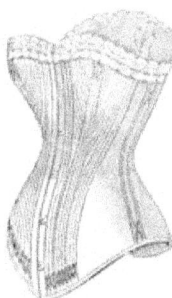

G. W. Poor, dealer in Dry and Fancy Goods, Graves' Block, Hudson, Mass.—So long as there are people who prefer merit to bluster and show, and prompt attention to delay and indifference, there will be a field for the operation of such enterprises as that carried on by Mr. G. W. Poor, Graves' Block, Hudson, dealer in dry and fancy goods. Immense "Dry Goods Emporiums," covering acres of space and containing crowds of people made up on the proportion of four "shoppers" to one buyer, may be delightful places to visit, but they are apt to get monotonous after a time, and a person whose moments are valuable, does not desire to spend the whole afternoon buying a yard or so of cloth. Therefore we take pleasure in calling attention to the store conducted by Mr. Poor. He handles dry and fancy goods very extensively, and assures prompt and courteous attention to every customer. Business was started about five years ago, and the retail trade has now reached large proportions, for the public have learned that the advantages offered at this store are genuine, and that entire confidence can be placed in all representations made. The premises occupied cover 1500 square feet. Three experienced and reliable assistants are employed who are courteous and polite in their attentions to all. Mr. Poor is ever on the alert to serve the interests of his patrons, and we take pleasure in commending this popular establishment.

Edgar B. Lucia, Registered Pharmacist, Rice's Block, opposite Town Hall, Hudson, Mass.—It is obvious that the entire community is interested in the question of obtaining pure and reliable drugs and medicines, for sickness is apt to appear in every family, and in spite of the claims made by those who argue in favor of "faith cure," most of us prefer to depend upon the means which the accumulated wisdom of thousands of years has placed at our disposal. Therefore such an establishment as that conducted by Mr. Edgar B. Lucia in Rice's Block, opposite the town hall, is worthy of hearty endorsement and support, for since Mr. Lucia began operations in 1888, he has proved to the satisfaction of all unprejudiced persons that he spares no pains to supply the most reliable drugs, medicines and chemicals obtainable in the market. As for his ability to choose and to dispense such agents, the fact of his being a registered pharmacist effectually establishes that point, leaving the record he has made for carefulness and skill entirely out of the question. A large stock is carried, comprising, in addition to the articles mentioned, a fine selection of druggist's sundries, toilet articles, confectionery, cigars, tobacco, etc. Prescriptions will be compounded in the most painstaking manner, and every facility is at hand to ensure perfect accuracy in the minutest details. Orders are promptly filled and the charges made are uniformly moderate. Mr. Lucia is a native of Putnam, Conn., and has gained a large circle of friends in Hudson and vicinity.

Graves & Jennison, Clothiers and Outfitters, Agents for the best Laundry in the Country, Hudson, Mass.—We all wish to look well and unless carried to extremes no one can find fault with this natural desire, which only springs from a proper self-respect and regard for the opinion of others. A powerful, and, in fact, the principal aid to presenting a good appearance is that given by well fitting and fashionable clothing, and hence it is not surprising that when the public discovers an establishment that gives them articles combining both these highly desirable qualities at low prices they should give it their hearty patronage and support. Such an enterprise is that carried on by Messrs. Graves & Jennison, which is located at No. 11 Main Street, Hudson, and the extent of their trade shows the appreciation of the public. Business was commenced in 1873 by Mr. H. W. Whitney, who was succeeded in 1876 by the present firm. Mr. A. K. Graves is a native of Southboro, Mass., but he is well known in this town, having been at different times selectman, overseer of the poor, treasurer and assessor. Mr. Jennison is a native of Wellesley, Mass., and served in the army for eighteen months. The premises are 24×75 feet in size. Their business as clothiers and outfitters is retail and they carry a fine assortment of all goods in that line, and an inspection of these goods will show that the workmanship is as honest as the goods are attractive. Trunks and bags can be found here, also, of best make and quality, and they are agents for the best laundry in the country.

L. D. Light, Board, Feed, Livery and Sale Stable, corner Park and Washington Streets, Hudson, Mass.—There are many reasons why such an establishment as that conducted by Mr. L. D. Light, at the corner of Park and Washington streets, is of benefit to the community, for a well managed livery, boarding and feed stable is a decided public convenience, inasmuch as it furnishes a means of enjoyable recreation and also tends to facilitate the operations of those visiting the town for business purposes. Mr. Light is a native of Maine, and has carried on his present enterprise for about six years. The premises utilized contain fourteen stalls, and horses taken to board are assured comfortable accommodations and intelligent care. Some very desirable teams are available for livery purposes, and as the charges are uniformly moderate, a fine opportunity is presented to those who enjoy a "spin on the road" behind a good horse. The vehicles are modern in style and are kept in the best of condition, while the horses are speedy and willing—quite different in fact, from those furnished by too many public stable keepers. Mr. Light has generally some very desirable animals on sale, and those wishing to purchase a good horse from a responsible party should give him a call.

C. E. Hall, manufacturer and dealer in every description of Harnesses; also dealer in Prof. J. A. Going's Valuable Horse Remedies, Saddles, Whips, Robes, Blankets, Sleigh Bells, Collars, all kinds of Horse Boots, Horse Brushes, Feather Dusters; Sperm, Neatsfoot, Machine, Axle and Harness Oil, Hudson, Mass.—Mr. C. E. Hall was born in Quincy, Mass., and has carried on operations in this town for nearly thirty years,

having founded his present business in 1860. Of course his establishment is one of the most widely known in this section, for no enterprise can be conducted for so long a period without gaining more than a local reputation, especially when, as in the case of that to which we have reference, its proprietor makes it a point to deal honorably with all and always to sell his goods strictly on their merits. Mr. Hall is a manufacturer of, and dealer in harness of every description, and those who appreciate the advantages of purchasing such goods from a reliable dealer would do well to give him a call when anything is wanted in the harness or horse furnishing line, for he carries a well-chosen stock made up of saddles, whips, robes, blankets, brushes, collars, all kinds of horse boots, horse brushes, feather dusters, etc., as well as sperm, neatsfoot, machine, axle and harness oils. The premises utilized are located on Main street, and are 28 × 36 feet in size, facilities being at hand for the making of custom work and the filling of orders for repairing at short notice, in a neat and durable manner. A full assortment of horse remedies is constantly on hand, and the prices quoted will be found uniformly reasonable.

Small Bros., dealers in all kinds of Salt and Fresh Fish, Oysters and Shell Fish. Orders delivered free in all parts of the Village. Chamberlain's Block, Wood Square, Hudson.—The manner in which some stores are managed makes it a wonder that any business is done in them at all, as their proprietors apparently proceed under the assumption that whatever service they may be called upon to render to their customers should be considered as a personal favor and not accepted as a right. In refreshing contrast to the above are the establishments run on true business principles in which a genuine spirit of accommodation prevails and prompt and courteous attention may be confidently expected by every patron, and it is of an example of the latter kind that we speak when referring to that conducted by Messrs. Small Bros., located in Chamberlain's Block, Wood Square, dealers in all kinds of fish. This enterprise was first started in 1887 by Greenhaw Bros., who were succeeded by W. E. Taylor, in 1888. The present proprietors assumed control in May, 1889, and carry on a growing wholesale and retail business in salt and fresh fish, also oysters and shell fish of all kinds. They occupy one floor measuring 20×40 feet, and employ a competent assistant. They are natives of Cape Cod, Mass., and although they have not been established in town so long a time as some others, they rank with our respected merchants. Those wishing anything in the fish line, and desiring strictly fresh and reliable goods at bottom prices would best serve their own interests by giving this enterprising firm a call. Orders are promptly attended to, and goods are delivered free to any part of the village. Messrs. Small Bros. ship lobsters and clams direct from Cape Cod, also their oysters direct from the beds, thereby saving middleman's profit, and ensuring to their customers products that are fresh and at the lowest possible market rates. Mr. W. H. Small of the above firm is the principal of the Hudson High School, in which capacity he is universally commended as a very efficient instructor.

Edw. F. Partridge, Pharmacist, Main Street, Hudson, Mass.— We are sure there are none of our readers in Hudson but what are acquainted with the enterprise conducted by Mr. Edw. F. Partridge, as pharmacist, located on Main street. There is no similar establishment in this vicinity, that is more popular or more worthy of popularity. This business was started in 1886 by Mr. Partridge, who makes it a point to keep his assortment of drugs, medicines, chemicals, etc., so full and complete as to be prepared to meet all demands that may be made upon it, and his careful attention to the interest of his customers has had its legitimate result in winning for him the esteem and confidence of the community. Callers at this store are received with uniform courtesy and served with care and promptness. The usual line of druggists' sundries are handled, including fancy and toilet articles, perfumery, etc. Mr. Partridge also carries a large assortment of his own preparations and the prices are as low as the nature of the article dealt in, will allow. Physicians' prescriptions are compounded with the utmost care and attention, and a liberal patronage is enjoyed in this department, as the public appreciate promptness combined with skill and caution. Only the purest ingredients are used and every effort is made to give complete satisfaction to all. The prices in this department are very reasonable, and form another reason for the increasing patronage which it receives.

HISTORICAL SKETCH

OF

FRAMINGHAM.

Like all the older townships of New England, Framingham has been reduced materially in area by the setting off of portions of her territory to form other towns, the reduction in the case of Framingham amounting to about twenty-five per cent, as the original plantation contained about 20,500 acres, while the present area of the town is 15,930 acres. The first reduction took place in 1715, some 500 acres, known as Simpson's Farm, being then included in the new town of Hopkinton. Holliston became possessed of a portion of the southern extremity of the town in 1724 ; and three years later Southborough took in "Fiddle Neck," as a certain long strip of land was called. In 1791 the "Leg" was annexed to Marlborough, and in 1846, a tract containing 3,000 acres was given up to form, in conjunction with parts of Hopkinton and Holliston, the town of Ashland. A small gain in territory was made in 1871, when a three-cornered piece of Natick land was annexed. Framingham lies half way between Boston and Worcester, being directly on the line, and is a beautiful as well as a prosperous town, its surface being agreeably varied, and the view from the higher lands being picturesque and attractive. On the north, adjoining the Sudbury line, is a range of high hills, the names of which are Nobscot, Doeskin Hill and Gibb's Mountain ; and in the Centre Village is Bare Hill, the summit of which commands an extensive and varied prospect, famous throughout this vicinity. Near the southern border are four clustered ponds, Cochituate Pond being on the eastern border and the Sudbury River flowing through the town diagonally from southwest to northeast. This river afforded abundant water-power before it was controlled by the city of Boston, and had much to do with the early building up of Framingham's industries. "The old Connecticut Path" passed through what was to become Framingham, and was first travelled in 1633 by a party of explorers journeying from Massachusetts Bay to the Connecticut Valley. Various Indian villages were located hereabouts, and the early history of the territory contains thrilling accounts of fights, massacres and other stirring events which characterized the relations of the white with the red men. The earliest records pertaining to this territory speak of it as "Wilderness Land lying north of the path from Sudbury to Nipnox;" this being afterward changed to "Waste Lands belonging to Thomas Danforth, Esq., lying between Marlbury and the old Connecticut Path." Finally by grant and by purchase Mr. Danforth became possessed of some two-thirds of the township, which was officially known as "Mr. Danforth's Farms" for many years.

WAVERLY BLOCK AND IRVING SQUARE, So. FRAMINGHAM.

He was born in Framlingham, England, and there is no doubt but that Framingham took its name from the English town, the "l" being dropped. Some have asserted that the original name was Framlingham, but there is no evidence to support this position other than that afforded by the insertion of the "l" in two instances in the county records. Mr. Danforth always omitted the "l" and certainly he should be deemed competent authority.

The first dwelling house was built in 1646, its site being near the river bank, half a mile north of the falls; the next one being erected in 1654, and several others within a few years from the latter date. King Philip's war put an end to settlement for a time but after the close of that struggle it was resumed on a comparatively large scale. The residents were connected with the church at Sudbury up to 1675, but after that time Framingham was known as a plantation, and incoming families were accredited to Sherborn, Marlborough, or Sudbury, according to where they settled, their property being assessed in the town to the meeting house of which it was the nearest. The first action in the direction of securing incorporation as a town was taken in 1693, when a petition was presented setting forth that its framers had lived on certain "remote lands" for nearly forty years, that the community was increasing steadily in numbers, that no meeting house was near, and that consequently the people were put to great inconvenience. This petition was not granted owing to the opposition of Sudbury and Sherborn, and another petition presented two years later was also refused, but the settlers were determined and persevering and finally secured the necessary act in 1700, seven years after their first attempt. Sherborn secured the insertion of a clause reserving to her certain rights, and this clause caused nine years of litigation ; brought about the double taxation of several families, and finally resulted in Sherborn being given 4000 acres of wild

LOOKING SOUTH FROM CONCORD STREET, So. FRAMINGHAM.

land by the legislature. The first church was organized and a pastor ordained in 1701 ; the first meeting house being located on the west bank of the Sudbury River, in the old cemetery. It was two stories high, 30 × 40 feet in dimensions and unpainted. With the exception of those on the front or south side, the windows were varied in size and position to suit individual pew owners, and doors were cut in the ends and rear of the building on the same accommodating plan.

Much of interest might be written concerning Framingham's conduct in the Revolution, for the town was patriotic and active throughout the war and her soldiers took a leading part in the Battle of Bunker Hill. Twenty-five Framingham men were killed in the war, and the total number of pensioners was sixty-five, fifteen of whom, or their widows, were living in 1840.

There were 1,500 inhabitants when the Revolution came to an end and for the next score of years very little increase was made. Comparatively speaking, the early facilities for education were very good, many of the first settlers being competent to act as teachers. Joshua Hemenway was employed as schoolmaster at an early date and received scholars in his house. The town was divided into five school districts in 1750, and school houses were built in the outskirts. The Framingham

Academy had its origin in 1792 and was regularly incorporated seven years later, being merged into the town high school in 1851. The State Normal School was opened in Lexington, in 1839, removed to West Newton in 1844 and to Framingham in 1853. In 1785 the proceeds of the sale of the last of the common lands, were devoted to the purchase of a public library and one has since been continuously maintained, various consolidations being effected from time to time, up to the establishment of the Framingham Town Library, in 1855. This is now one of the best equipped town libraries in the State.

The present importance of Framingham is of course due to the extent and diversity of her manufacturing interests, which have attained great magnitude within comparatively few years. South Framingham is the headquarters for the industrial and mercantile interests of the town, and it is worthy of note that the first village industry of more than local importance was the manufacture of straw bonnets and was begun in 1815. Although straw goods manufacturing has attained great magnitude here, it is now but one of various very extensive lines of industry. The South Village is the central station of the Boston & Albany Railroad, which of course has very materially aided its growth, but since the opening of the Boston & Albany in 1835, various other roads have been built, making the village an important railroad centre.

The South Framingham Post-Office was established February 12, 1841, the original postmaster having been Joseph Fuller. Saxonville, another important manufacturing village, is treated of in another portion of this book. The industrial development of Framingham has been interfered with to some extent by the seizure of Sudbury River, as an additional water supply by the city of Boston, but there seems to be no reason to fear any further interruptions and it is evident that the manufacturing enterprises of the town are founded on a basis of solid prosperity. Recognizing that the limitations of space have prevented us from doing justice to Framingham's history, we feel the less regret from the fact that the action of the town in publishing a History and Genealogical Register, in 1887, has placed it within the power of all interested to thoroughly familiarize themselves with the subject. The task was entrusted to the Rev. G. H. Temple, the author of several town histories, and a man thoroughly well fitted, both by nature and by education, for the work assigned him. He has produced a history which is strictly reliable, broad in scope and interesting in treatment, and we acknowledge our obligations to it for facts set forth in our own brief and imperfect record.

LEADING BUSINESS MEN

SO. FRAMINGHAM, MASS.

A. R. Newton & Son, House Furnishers, Furniture, Carpets, Stoves, Wall Paper, Window Shades, Upholstered Goods, Waverly Block, South Framingham, Mass.—The enterprise conducted by Messrs. A. R. Newton & Son was inaugurated by Messrs. Bacon & Yates, this firm being succeeded by Messrs. S. Yates & Co. in 1882, and the present proprietors assuming control in 1888. The firm is composed of Messrs. A. R. and F. B. Newton, both of whom are natives of South Framingham and are very generally known here. The premises occupied are located in Waverly Block and comprise three floors and a storeroom, their total area, exclusive of the latter apartment, being over 9000 square feet, having been much enlarged since the first of last year. The firm rank with the most enterprising and reliable house furnishers doing business in this section of the State, buying for cash they offer goods at the very lowest rates. The stock carried is remarkable alike for completeness and variety. It comprises furniture, carpets, stoves, wall paper, window shades, upholstered goods, etc., and contains so wide a range of thoroughly dependable articles that all tastes as well as all purses can be easily suited. The question of price has so all-important a bearing upon the success or failure of a business enterprise that the mere fact of this concern's doing so large a business as it does is of itself enough to show that bottom figures are quoted, and indeed it is perfectly safe to assert that, quality for quality, no retail house in the State names lower figures on the goods handled. Every article sold here is guaranteed to prove as represented, the latest novelties in house furnishings as well as full lines of staple goods are at hand to choose from and three competent and polite assistants are employed, prompt and painstaking attention being assured every caller. Orders are delivered at short notice and without charge. No trouble is spared to fully satisfy the most critical customers.

Burtis Judd, Real Estate and Insurance Agent. Farms, Village and Country Residences for Sale, Mortgages Negotiated, Tenements to Rent and Rents Collected, Fire Insurance Effected at the Lowest Rates in the Best Companies, Office Waverly Block, South Framingham, Mass.—The gentleman whose card we print above, is one of the best known business men carrying on operations in South Framingham and vicinity, for the nature of his calling brings him into contact with all classes of people, and during the twelve years that he has been located in this section and pursued his present occupation, he has gained many friends and built up a most enviable reputation for integrity, ability and promptness. Mr. Judd was born in Bethel, Conn., and began operations here in South Framingham in 1877. He is extensively engaged in handling real estate and always has on his books such a variety of farms, village and country residences, that those wishing to purchase anything in this line will save time and trouble by giving him a call. The estates offered by him vary greatly in price, size, location, etc., and therefore all tastes and all means can generally be suited from the list at hand. Mr. Judd, who has many desirable tenements to rent, and collects rent for property owners who do not care to give personal attention to such duties. He is also prepared to effect fire insurance at the lowest rates in some of the leading companies, among which may be mentioned the following :

Abington Mutual, Quincy Mutual, Fitchburg Mutual, Merrimac Mutual, Dorchester Mutual, Continental Insurance Co., Glens Falls Insurance Co., Williamsburg Insurance Co., Jersey City Insurance Co., Rutgers Insurance Co., Sun Fire Office, London, England.

Mr. Judd's office is in Waverly Block, and prompt and courteous attention is assured to every caller. He has placed a great deal of insurance for property owners hereabouts and offers advantages equal to the best.

S. H. Williams, Planing Mill, Saw Mill, and Packing Box Manufactory, Marble Street, South Framingham, Mass.—Very few people, not immediately interested, have any idea of the extent to which the manufacture of packing boxes is carried on, and it would unquestionably surprise the large majority of our readers should they visit the establishment conducted by Mr. S. H. Williams, on Marble street, and see the magnitude of the preparations made to carry on this line of production alone. Mr. Williams sells packing boxes directly to manufacturers, and operates one of the best equipped factories of the kind in New England, enabling him to fill the heaviest orders at short notice and to quote the lowest market rates at all times. The business was founded in 1870 by Messrs. Fales & Williams, and at first included carpentering and building, mill work, etc., but when the partnership was dissolved in 1875, Mr. Williams took up his present line of work. He carries on a first class planing mill and saw mill in connection with the production of packing boxes, and occupies a three-story and a basement building, of the dimensions of 40×115 feet, the upper floor being utilized by the Framingham Box Manufacturing Co. The engine-house is quite distinct from the main building, being separated from it by a double brick wall, thus reducing the risk of fire very materially. Employment is given to twenty-six men, and the value of the yearly product reaches a very high figure.

C. O. Trowbridge, dealer in Dry and Fancy Goods, Ladies' and Gents' Boots and Shoes, Flour, Grain, Groceries, Crockery and Glass Ware, Paper Hangings and Wooden Ware, Framingham, Mass.—Whether it is in the extent, variety, or general desirability, of the stock carried, it would be hard to surpass the showing made by Mr. C. O. Trowbridge, located in Framingham, Mass., for the proprietor is a man of no small experience in the handling of the goods in which he deals, and he spares no effort to supply his customers with the best the market affords in sufficient variety to suit all tastes. This establishment was originally started by Messrs. Alderman & Co., who were succeeded in 1879 by Messrs. Trowbridge & Savage, and in 1884 Mr. C. O. Trowbridge, the present proprietor, assumed full control of the business, and although it is unusual, even in this prosperous community for so large a patronage as he has attained to be built up in so short a time, still there is, after all, but little to wonder at in his success, for, as we have before remarked, he is a man of experience, and believes in honorable, liberal methods of conducting business. The public was quick to perceive the inducements held out, and therefore extended hearty and continuous support to the undertaking. The proprietor is a native of Framingham and is overseer of the poor, and is very favorably known throughout the community. The premises occupied comprise two stories and a basement each 40×60 feet in dimensions and employment is given to three competent and polite assistants. A large stock is carried of useful and fancy novelties general y to be found in a first class variety store, such as dry and fancy goods, ladies' and gents' boots and shoes, flour, grain, groceries, crockery and glass ware, paper hangings and wooden ware. Strong inducements are here extended, and every effort is made to handle only reliable articles at bottom prices.

Wm. W. Haynes, dealer in Watches, Clocks and Jewelry, Silver and Plated Wares, Spectacles, etc., Nobscot Block, in Store with Dr. Rice, South Framingham, Mass.—A reliable watch is without doubt as useful a companion as a man can have in these days, when business is done on the "high pressure" system, and the missing of a train or the failure to keep an engagement with one whose minutes are worth dollars and who cannot therefore afford to wait for a haggard, may seriously injure one's prospects. Happily there is nothing to hinder practically all who would profit by punctuality from possessing an accurate timekeeper, for, as a visit to the establishment conducted by Mr. Wm. W. Haynes will show, such an article may now be bought for very little money. Mr. Haynes, who occupies a store in Nobscot Block in conjunction with Dr. Rice, carries a full line of watches in gold and silver cases, and quotes the lowest market rates on fully warranted goods. He also deals largely in clocks, jewelry, silver and plated ware, spectacles, etc., and offers some very desirable novelties in each of these lines. The repairing of watches, clocks and jewelry is given immediate and skillful attention, no exorbitant charges being made and all work being strictly guaranteed. Mr. Haynes has carried on this enterprise for five years and is well and favorably known.

J. F. ROACH,
Carriage, Sign and Ornamental Painter,

Howard St., South Framingham, Mass.

BOX 767.

The enterprise carried on by Mr. J. F. Roach, on Howard street, was formerly conducted by Messrs. Roach & Bryant, the present proprietor assuming sole control at the beginning of the year 1889. He is a native of Framingham, and is so generally known in this vicinity that extended personal mention is hardly necessary. Mr. Roach occupies premises of the dimensions of 40×70 feet and has every facility at hand for the doing of carriage, sign and ornamental painting in the most approved manner and at reasonable rates. He employs four competent assistants, and is in a position to fill orders at very short notice if desired. Using selected stock, employing skilled workmen and giving careful personal supervision to the many details of his business, it is but natural that Mr. Roach should turn out work fully equal to the best. Poor painting, and especially poor *carriage* painting, is neither useful, durable nor ornamental and both trouble and money may be saved by placing orders for anything in this line with so thoroughly competent and reputable a business man as Mr. Roach. He deals in new and second-hand carriages and harness to a considerable extent, and though he carries no stock, is in a position to offer some special inducements to those wishing to buy anything of the kind.

F. B. Horne, Druggist, Framingham, Mass.— It is perfectly natural that the public should prefer an establishment in which prompt attention and uniform courtesy are extended to every caller, and therefore it is not surprising that Mr. F. B. Horne's drug store should be one of the most popular in this section of the State. The premises utilized measure 20×50 feet and are nicely and conveniently arranged, a very large stock being carried, and every provision made to ensure precision in the filling of orders. Drugs, medicines and chemicals of all descriptions are kept on hand in sufficient quantities to supply every demand, and great pains is taken to ensure their purity and general excellence. Mr. Horne is a native of Framingham and has been identified with his business since 1876. He is a thoroughly competent pharmacist and gives particular attention to the compounding of physicians' prescriptions, rightly estimating this the most important department of his business. Although the main point looked after is accuracy, speed is by no means lost sight of, and annoying waits are avoided by patronizing this establishment. The prices are made as low as is compatible with the furnishing of fine and fresh articles, and will compare very favorably with those quoted at any other first-class pharmacy. Toilet articles, stationery and confectionery are also handled to considerable extent, and it is necessary to employ competent assistants in order to serve all patrons with promptness and politeness at this establishment.

W. C. CHAMBERLIN,

DENTIST,

CENTRAL BLOCK,

(Over Hastings Clothing Store.)

SOUTH FRAMINGHAM, - MASS.

Whitmore & Daboll, dealers in Tea, Coffee, Flour, Sugar, Spices, Butter, Cheese, Eggs, Lard, etc., Waverly Street, South Framingham.— Without doubt one of the best known and most popular of the many grocery stores located in South Framingham and vicinity is that carried on by Messrs. Whitmore & Daboll, and when the methods pursued by the firm in question are taken into consideration, we believe no further explanation will be needed of how this popularity has been attained. The enterprise was inaugurated in 1885 by F. E. Whitmore, the present firm assuming control in 1887. It is composed of Messrs. F. E. Whitmore and C. M. Daboll, both of whom give careful personal attention to the carrying on of affairs, and with the aid of two efficient assistants assure immediate and careful service to every customer. The premises made use of are located on Waverly street, and comprise one floor and a basement of the dimensions of 20×50 feet. The stock is both large and varied, and includes tea, coffee, flour, sugar, spices, butter, cheese, eggs, lard, crockery, glass ware and other commodities too numerous to mention. The goods are dependable, the prices are low and orders are accurately delivered at short notice. Therefore the firm do a large business, which is bound to steadily increase so long as the present methods are adhered to.

Boston Shoe Store, J. F. McGlenan, Fine Boots, Shoes, Rubbers and Gents' Furnishing Goods, Waverly Block, South Framingham, Mass.—Among those bits of miscellaneous information which are sure to "come in handy" to everybody at one time or another, the whereabouts of a well managed retail boot and shoe store may properly be classed. All of us wear boots or shoes, and practically all of us like to know where we can obtain anything in this line at the lowest market rates, and for this reason the following brief mention of the facilities by Mr. J. F. McGlenan the proprietor of the "Boston Shoe Store" will be of interest, for this gentleman not only quotes bottom prices but offers as fine a stock of footwear to choose from as any one could wish to see. The enterprise was formerly carried on by Messrs. J. F. McGlenan & Co., but in 1888, the present owner assumed entire control. He is a native of Providence, R. I., and has had sufficient experience in connection with his present line of business to be thoroughly conversant with it in every detail. The store is located in Waverly Block, at the corner of Waverly and Hollis streets, and has an area of 1200 square feet. The stock on hand comprises boots, shoes and rubbers of every description as well as a fine line of gents' furnishing goods, and those in search of the latest novelties as well as those who prefer more staple goods, can find what they want here and may be sure of getting it at the lowest market rates in every instance. The goods are warranted to prove as represented, and customers are attended to without delay.

Mrs. S. S. Given, Ladies' and Gents' Dining Rooms, 11 Waverly Street, South Framingham, Mass.—Mrs. S. S. Given has carried on the enterprise with which she is now connected since 1875, having at that date succeeded Mr. L. P. Wood. She is a native of Boston, and has a large circle of friends in South Framingham and vicinity. The ladies' and gents' dining rooms conducted by her, are located at No. 11 Waverly street, and have a most enviable reputation, for the food is first-class, the cooking is of the best and the service is neat, prompt and efficient. Mrs. Given offers a varied and carefully arranged bill of fare, and there is certainly no reason why all tastes cannot be suited from the extensive list presented. She also rents rooms at moderate rates, and such of our readers as may have occasion to make a long or short stay in this town and do not care to go to the expense, or wish to avoid the inevitable publicity attendant upon putting up at a hotel, would do well to take advantage of the accommodations offered by Mrs. Given, and we are sure that should they do so, they will have reason to thank us for the hint here given. The rooms are pleasantly situated, comfortably furnished and well kept. Employment is given to three assistants and guests are assured prompt and polite attention.

Geo. J. Masterson, Confectioner, Fruit, Cigars, Tobacco and Pastry, Concord Street, South Framingham, Mass.—There are some people who appear to have as strong a dislike for confectionery as a mad dog has of water, for they are always warning others not to eat candies or sweets of any kind and evidently regard sugar as a mild form of poison. Nothing could be much more nonsensical, for the fact that sugar is present in almost all kinds of food is of itself enough to show that it is beneficial and that its reasonable use is necessary to health. There is some confectionery which is hurtful, no doubt, owing to adulteration or improper flavoring, but there is no danger of being supplied with such if a reputable dealer be patronized. Mr. George J. Masterson, doing business on Concord street, is one of the best known confectioners in this town and has won an enviable reputation for supplying his customers with delicious and wholesome goods at moderate rates. He was born here in South Framingham, and has carried on his present enterprise since 1888. The premises utilized are 15×30 feet in dimensions, and contain not only a fine assortment of fresh confectionery, but also fruit, pastry, cigars, tobacco, etc. Employment is given to three assistants and customers may depend upon receiving prompt and courteous attention. Mr. Masterson guarantees his goods to prove as represented, and as his prices are uniformly low it is natural that he should enjoy an extensive patronage.

Fig 1   *Fig 2*

T. Wise Motor and Machine Co., Wise's Patent Steam Fan Blower for Hot or Cold Blast, rear Liberty Block, South Framingham, Mass.— It is now some eight years since Wise's Patent Steam Fan Blower was placed upon the market, and we believe that it cannot be successfully disputed that the claims made for it by Mr. Thomas Wise, the inventor, at the time of its introduction, have been proved to be fully justified by the facts. The blower is run without the use of belts or a steam engine, it being driven by steam taken directly from the boiler, from eight to ten pounds pressure being sufficient It requires no special foundation, is compact and simple in construction, and can be used to advantage in positions where any other style of fan blower could not possibly give satisfaction These blowers are made in different sizes and are fully warranted to prove just as represented. They are now being manufactured and sold by the T. Wise Motor and Machine Company, of which Mr. Thomas Wise is manager. He was born in Boston and is also the inventor of a steam motor for driving an electric dynamo without engine or belting, for the lighting of cars, steam boats, public buildings, etc., and is prepared to give any desired information relative to this appliance on application. The company occupy premises in the rear of Liberty Block, and give prompt and careful attention to orders for their specialties, and for steam-heating apparatus and iron-piping of all kinds. Heating plants will be put up and guaranteed to work satisfactorily, and moderate charges are made in every instance

---

Thomson Brothers, Horse-Shoeing and Carriage Work, Howard Street, South Framingham, Mass.—This firm was formed August 4, 1889, Mr. H. H. Thomson, the senior brother, having previously conducted the wheelwright and carriage business at the same stand, having succeeded Mr. E. Wilkinson, at the above date. Mr. A. W. Thomson became a partner, the firm purchasing the blacksmith business of Mr. W. H. Daniels, since which both branches of the business have been carried on by the firm occupying the premises measuring 30 × 60 feet and are located on Howard street, and are fitted up with all necessary facilities for the making of carriages and wagons to order, and the doing of repairing at short notice in a thorough and workmanlike manner, and blacksmithing and shoeing is done in first-class manner. Thomson Brothers have built up quite an extensive trade, for they are very careful and skillful workmen and allow no inferior work to leave their shop at any price, they evidently believe there are but two ways of turning out jobs—a right way and a wrong way —and spare no pains to combine strength, neatness and " good style " in all these operations. Cheap and inferior carriage or wagon work is sure to prove the most costly in the long run, and that this fact is very generally appreciated in this vicinity, is shown by the rapidly growing popularity of the shop to which we have reference. Thomson Bros. make no exorbitant charges, but quote as low rates as are consistent with the use of selected material and skilled labor.

A. J. Wood, Millinery and Fancy Goods, East Waverly Block, South Framingham, Mass.— Among those establishments which are fairly entitled to being ranked as representative in their respective lines, the two conducted by Miss A. J. Wood in East Waverly Block, Waverly street, must be given prominent mention, for the enterprise carried on by this lady was inaugurated some eighteen years ago and has long been held in high estimation by that portion of the public interested in millinery, fancy goods, etc. Operations were begun by Miss L. Dowse, in 1871, she being succeeded by the present owner in 1874. The other store, devoted to dry goods and small wares was formerly carried on by Mr. Wm. McNulty, Miss Wood succeeding him in 1889. Miss Wood is a native of Upton, Mass, and has a very extensive acquaintance in South Framingham and vicinity. Her exceptional taste in the selection and arrangement of millinery goods, etc., is so generally conceded and has had so pronounced an influence in building up her business, that it is unnecessary for us to dwell upon it, suffice it to say that its effects are plainly noticeable in the character of the stock offered and the nature of the order work turned out at her establishment. The premises occupied have an area of 700 square feet in the millinery store and about 1400 in the dry goods store, and her stocks contain a most attractive assortment of millinery and fancy goods, foreign and domestic dry goods and small wares, comprising the very latest and most tasteful novelties. Moderate prices are quoted in every department, and the prompt and polite attention given to callers has no little to do with the store's popularity. Order work is made a specialty, and as eight competent assistants are employed, commissions can be executed at short notice in a most satisfactory manner.

Geo. F. Bemis, Watches and Clocks Cleaned and Repaired, Framingham, Mass.—A house which probably carries at least as full an assortment of the goods in which it deals as any similar establishment in this village is that now conducted by Mr. Geo. F. Bemis. This gentleman succeeded Mr. Cyrus N. Gibbs in business in 1881, and has been successful in building up a reputation for honest and faithful work in all grades of work in his line. Mr. Bemis keeps a good line of the daily and weekly papers, and periodicals, which is an accommodation to this vicinity. The jewelry repairing department is a very important feature of the business, a specialty being made of repairing. Most complicated and delicate watches or chronometers may be unhesitatingly confided to Mr. Bemis with the assurance that they cannot be entrusted to more skillful or experienced hands. Repairs of whatever nature in watches, clocks, jewelry, etc., will receive early and painstaking attention and will be executed at very low prices. Mr. Bemis was born in Shrewsbury, Mass., and served in the United States Navy for twelve years. He is well known throughout Framingham, as an enterprising and reliable man, and one who can safely guarantee that all work in his particular line that is entrusted to him shall be satisfactorily performed in every particular.

W. F. Ward, Meat, Canned Goods, Fruit, Vegetables, Grant Street, South Framingham, Mass.—There is nothing to be gained by stinting one's self in the matter of food, and this fact is now so clearly demonstrated that there should be an end to the clamors of those good-intentioned but unpractical men who have had so much to say in the past about the "extravagance" of American working-men who eat a good deal of meat and insist upon having it of superior quality too. They no doubt eat more solid food than do workingmen across the water, but they also do more solid work and consequently there is a distinct gain instead of that "tremendous loss" we all have heard so much about. The great demand for meats, etc., has resulted in many establishments devoted to their sale being opened in this vicinity, and prominent among these is that conducted by Mr. W. F. Ward, located on Grant street. Mr. Ward is extremely well known in South Framingham, and occupies the position of overseer of the poor. The premises made use of by him are of the dimensions of 25×35 feet, and are well stocked with a carefully selected assortment of meats, canned goods, vegetables, fruits, etc. This assortment is sufficiently varied to allow of all tastes and purses being suited, and the goods composing it are quoted at the lowest market rates in every instance. Mr. Ward has built up a very desirable trade since beginning operations in 1888, and his establishment owes a good share of its popularity to the care and promptness shown in the filling of every order.

F. C. Hastings, One Price Clothier, dealer in Men's and Boys' Fine Ready Made Clothing, Hats and Furnishings, Trunks and Bags, Hollis Street, South Framingham, Mass.—Mr. F. C. Hastings shows a very desirable stock of fine ready-made clothing at his store on Hollis street, and those who wish to purchase anything in this line will make no mistake if they place their orders with him, first because his garments are fully up to the standard in every respect, and second because they are offered at the lowest market rates. Mr. Hastings is a native of Framingham and has carried on his present establishment since 1882. His reputation for square dealing is too well known to require dwelling upon in these pages, and the genuine character of the inducements offered to customers has resulted in the building up of a large business. Another thing which has done much to bring the enterprise favorably before the public is the uniform courtesy shown to every caller, whether you wish to buy or merely to "look around," you are assured prompt and polite attention, and should you make a purchase it will prove as represented every time. Hats and furnishings are dealt in as well as clothing, as are also trunks, bags and similar goods. The latest and most approved novelties are obtained at the earliest possible moment, and those who make it a point to be fully "up to the times" in their dress, will gain many valuable hints by visiting this popular establishment.

One Price Shoe Store, Concord Street, South Framingham, Mass.—The "one price shoe store" is probably as generally popular an institution as could easily be found in this vicinity, and the causes of its popularity are by no means hard to discover, for it only needs a visit to the establishment to demonstrate that the stock on hand is large, varied and most skillfully selected, that the prices quoted are as low as the lowest (being put down to hard pan to begin with and not so arranged that they may be "beaten down" ten or twenty per cent and still yield a profit) and that callers are sure of receiving prompt and polite attention. Of course, under these circumstances the enterprise is bound to be popular, and to constantly increase in popularity under its present methods of management. It was started in 1880 by Mr. James Sullivan, who, since 1887 has carried it on in partnership with Mr. A. J. Hemenway. Both these gentlemen are natives of this town and have many friends in the community. Boots, shoes, rubbers and in fact footwear of all kinds are constantly in stock, repairing of every description is promptly, neatly and strongly done at moderate rates, and no one in want of anything in their line of business can afford to pass by the advantages offered by this energetic and experienced firm.

Wm. Nicholson, Florist. P. O. Box 265, Framingham, Mass.—It is very interesting to observe how plants and flowers may be influenced and helped or hindered in their growth by skillful cultivation, and the nearest that man has come to ever creating anything is doubtless in this field of operation. Blossoms are now grown single, double or triple, at the will of the florist, colors are mingled and shaded to suit the taste, and new varieties of flowers are constantly being produced. Of course to accomplish such wonderful things in our unfavorable northern climate, requires elaborate and costly hot-houses and other apparatus as well as experience and skill, and considering the necessary expenses that florists are put to, it is surprising that they are able to supply their productions at the generally low rates quoted by them. There is, to be sure, considerable difference in the prices asked by different houses in this business, but no mistake can be made in placing orders with Mr. Wm. Nicholson as this gentleman bears a well-earned reputation for supplying plants and flowers at the lowest market rates. The greenhouses now managed by Mr. Nicholson were started by Mr. W. H. Mellen in 1880 as private ones, and in 1887 Mr. Nicholson hired the estate of the Mellen heirs, and the undertaking has been received with unusual favor, as it at once became apparent that the proprietor had a thorough knowledge of his business, and was well prepared to meet all honorable competition. The conservatories cover an area of 6000 square feet and are heated by hot water, and comprise one house devoted to the cultivation of roses, one to carnations, and two to the raising of tomatoes and cucumbers. Wholesale or retail orders addressed to P. O. Box 165, Framingham, Mass., for either of the above named flowers or vegetables will receive prompt attention, and will be supplied at positively the lowest market rates. Mr. Nicholson is about building a new and large green house for the accommodation of all his rapidly increasing business which will be located on Cross street between Grove and Pleasant streets within three minutes' walk from Framingham Centre depot. He expects to move his business to this new plant about September 1, 1890. A full line of budding plants constantly on hand, and orders for hardy shrubs and roses will be filled promptly.

C. C. Stevens, dealer in Ice. Refrigerators for Sale or to Let. Office: No. 1 Concord Street, near railroad crossing. Ice Houses: Learned Street, off Union Avenue, South Framingham, Mass.—It was formerly supposed that the process of freezing eliminated all impurities from the water, and that consequently all fresh water ice was suitable for family use no matter from what source it came. Comparatively recent experiments and analyses have proved this theory to be false, however, and as the dangers arising from the promiscuous use of impure ice are similar in kind if not in degree to those incurred by using impure water, we feel we are doing our readers a service by calling their attention to them and by showing how they may be avoided. Mr. C. C. Stevens makes a specialty of dealing in pure ice and is prepared to supply it in any desired quantities at moderate rates. His ice-houses are located on Learned street, off Union avenue, on Leonard's pond which is a spring-supplied pond affording water of the very highest test of purity, and have a capacity of 7,000 tons, so that even his extensive wholesale and retail trade can be fully accommodated. Mr. Stevens was born in Lebanon, Maine, and succeeded Mr. Edwin Eames in the ownership of the business under consideration in in 1876. He was at one time road commissioner and is very generally known throughout this section. The system of delivery is well-arranged, and as experienced, careful and courteous drivers are employed, customers may depend upon reliable and uniformly satisfactory service. Mr. Stevens has refrigerators for sale or to let and supplies them at low rates. His office is at No. 1 Concord street, near railroad crossing, and callers will receive immediate and polite attention.

Edmonds & Brown, Hurlburt's old stand; Jewellers and Opticians; constantly on hand a fine line of Watches, Clocks, Jewelry and Silverware; Irving Square, South Framingham, Mass.—This establishment was founded in 1878 by Mr. W. R. Hurlbut who continued the business until 1889 when it passed into the possession of the present firm. The store is located in Irving square, and carries a carefully chosen stock of jewelry, watches, clocks, silver and plated ware, together with a fine assortment of spectacles and eye glasses of all kinds. All these goods are fully warranted to prove precisely as represented, and the prices quoted on them will bear the severest comparison with any named on articles of equal merit elsewhere; a specialty is made of fine repairing and jobbing, and those wishing to have anything in the jewelry line made to order, will find Messrs. Edmonds & Brown ready to execute such commissions in a superior manner at moderate rates. The most delicate and difficult repairing will be skillfully done at short notice, watches being cleaned, oiled and put in perfect running order at small expense.

Gregory & Co., Boot and Shoe manufacturers, South Framingham, Mass.—The enterprise now conducted under the firm-name of Gregory & Co., was inaugurated nearly seventy years ago, it having been originally established in 1821. Thirty years later it came into the possession of Messrs. Claflin, Coburn & Co., who were succeeded by the firm of Bridges & Co. in 1876. In 1890 the firm-name was changed to Gregory & Co., the Boston office is at No. 138 Summer street. Ex Governor W. Claflin, N. P. Coburn, James A. Woolson, Wm. F. Gregory and O. B. Root are the proprietors. Mr. D. T. Bridges is the manager of the South Framingham factory. This gentleman is a native of Hopkinton and gives close personal attention to the more important details connected with the carrying on of the enterprise. The factory is five stories in height and 40×240 feet in dimensions, being equipped with the latest improved machinery in every department, the total capacity of the plant being 2400 pairs per day. Employment is given to 375 operatives, and a seventy-five-horse engine is utilized to furnish the necessary motive power. The productions of this vast establishment have been so long accepted as the standard in their various lines that it is quite unnecessary to dwell upon their desirability, but it may at least be said that no trouble is spared to fully maintain their unsurpassed reputation, and that no firm in the country is better prepared to fill the heaviest orders at positively bottom rates.

Wm. J. Arbuckle, Horseshoer, Carriage Smith, and General Jobber, South Framingham, Mass.—Mr. Wm. J. Arbuckle succeeded Mr. O. N. Callahan at the beginning of 1889, but he is by no means inexperienced in the horse-shoeing and carriage smithing business, having carried it on for a full score of years in Boston, Walpole, etc. He is a native of West Medway, Mass., and has an extended "war record," having served in the army five years and six months. His shop is located west of the Common, and has an area of 2000 square feet, being fitted up with every facility for the making of carriages and wagons to order, and the doing of jobbing of all kinds.

Mr. Arbuckle employs three efficient assistants, and as he gives personal attention to the filling of orders, is well prepared to warrant all work leaving his shop. Those thinking of having a wagon or carriage built would do well to communicate with him, for estimates will be promptly and cheerfully furnished and his experience enables him to produce vehicles combining good stock and good workmanship, at moderate figures. Repairing is neatly and durably done at short notice, and no pains is spared to fully satisfy every customer, and to abide closely by all representations and agreements which may be made, thus building up a large business on a firm and sure foundation.

Tucker & Young, Real Estate Brokers, Odd Fellows Block, Managers South Framingham, Mass., Branch Office of the Co-operative Farm Agency. (Main Office, 178 Washington Street, Boston, Mass.)—The South Framingham branch of the Co-operative Farm Agency, whose main office is at No. 178 Washington street, Boston, was opened by Mr. J. M. Young in January, 1889, and during the same year the firm was changed to Tucker & Young. The concern transact a general insurance business representing some of best fire insurance companies. They are also agents for the Mutual Life Insurance Company. They handle real estate of all kinds, and those who wish to buy or to sell anything in this line, will find it for their interest to give the firm a call, for the time thus spent will not be wasted at all events, for Messrs. Tucker & Young are in a position to give "inside" information concerning real estate matters and offer so large a variety of such property that there are but few investors who could not find something on their books suited to their taste and means. Money will be loaned on real estate at moderate rates, and perhaps some of our readers who are in want of cash or who think that the interest they are now paying is higher than it should be, may make arrangements advantageous to all parties concerned by stating their case to Messrs. Tucker & Young. The experiment is worth trying, and we need hardly add that such business is considered strictly confidential.

South Framingham Hotel, Wm. G. Morse, Proprietor. Terms, $2.00 per day. Special rates to commercial men. Opposite the Depot, South Framingham, Mass.—There is no lack of hotels in South Framingham and each of them no doubt has its merits, but it would be difficult to find one more generally and deservedly popular among experienced travellers than is that conducted by Mr. William G. Morse, opposite the depot. The South Framingham Hotel has been carried on by the present proprietor for about fifteen years, and is a twenty-five room house, offering about as much "solid comfort" to the square inch as any hotel we know of. Mr. Morse served in the army during the Rebellion, and is so widely known in this vicinity that detailed personal mention of him is entirely uncalled for. That he "knows how to keep a hotel" hundreds of people will cheerfully testify, and his popularity among "commercial men" is by no means the least convincing proof of his abilities in this respect, for these wide awake members of the community are certainly well qualified to judge of the merits of a hotel, and are as outspoken in denouncing a house that is not managed as it should be, as they are generous in patronizing one which is carried on in the liberal and intelligent manner which characterizes the management of the South Framingham Hotel. The terms of this house are $2.00 per day, and special rates are made to commercial men. The rooms are pleasant, comfortably furnished and well kept, and the table is supplied at all times of year with an abundant variety of wholesome and palatable food. Employment is given to six efficient assistants, and the service is uniformly prompt and reliable.

Auburn Last Co., manufacturers of Lasts of All Kinds and Sole Patterns. E. D. Stone, Treasurer and Superintendent, Factory on Howard Street, South Framingham, Mass.—The Auburn Last Company began operations in 1876 and was at that time located in Auburn, Maine, but in 1882 the business was transferred to this town, since when its rapid and constant development has proved the wisdom of the change. The factory is a two-story structure of the dimensions of 30×50 feet, and is equipped with a very complete plant of the most improved machinery, power being furnished by a twenty-five-horse engine. The company manufacture lasts of every description and also sole patterns, their productions being so well and favorably known to manufacturers as to render detailed mention entirely unnecessary. A specialty is made of rubber shoe lasts, and the prices quoted on these goods afford a significant indication of the degree of economy of production which may be brought about by the use of efficient machinery, the employment of skilled labor, and painstaking and intelligent superintendence. The most extensive orders can be filled at short notice and the lowest market rates are named on all the goods produced. The treasurer and superintendent is Mr. E. D. Stone, who is a native of Falmouth, Maine, and has an extensive acquaintance among boot and shoe manufacturers. He gives very careful supervision to the many details of the business and the company's high reputation is largely due to his efforts to fully satisfy every customer.

J. H. Randall, House Painter and Decorator, Hard Wood Polishing, Tinting, Whitening and Paper Hanging, Framingham Centre, Mass. Post-office Box 11, South Framingham, Mass.— Economy is an excellent thing in its way; but there is a decided difference between true and false economy, and care should be taken lest in seeking one the other should be fallen into. For instance, it used to be the custom to allow buildings to remain unpainted to save the expense of painting them, but it has been discovered by experience that such a course, far from saving money actually wasted it, as the elements beating on the bare boards soon reduced them to decay and uselessness. It therefore follows that no frame structure should be permitted to be exposed, wholly or in part, without the protection afforded by paint, and considerations of economy, as well as of pride, should induce every house-owner to see that his buildings are thoroughly covered with this useful material. It will not require frequent renewing if applied by skillful hands, and as good a firm as can be found to attend to work of the kind, is that of J. H. Randall, doing business on Main street. This firm commenced operations in 1889, and has gained the confidence and patronage of the public by the use of first-class stock, and the prompt and careful filling of all orders. The premises occupied cover an area of 1350 feet, where Mr. Randall is prepared to receive orders for all kinds of house and decorative painting, also glazing, sign painting, paper hanging, tinting, kalsomining and white-washing, etc. A sufficient force of competent workmen are employed to guarantee all work to be satisfactory, and done in a neat, clean, and workmanlike manner. Orders by mail addressed to post-office box No. 11, South Framingham, Mass., will be acted upon without delay, and the lowest prices are charged that are consistent with fine material, and skilled labor. Mr. Randall is a thoroughly practical workman and gives close personal attention to all the details of his business.

Isaac A. Lombard, Pharmacist; also Circulating Library, South Framingham, Mass.—The oldest pharmacy in town is that conducted by Mr. Isaac A. Lombard, on Waverly street, and this establishment deserves especially prominent mention for other reasons than that of its long standing, for there is no similar enterprise in this vicinity carried on in a more accommodating and yet conservative style. The proprietor is a native of South Framingham, and began operations here in 1870. He is very widely known throughout this section and his abilities as a well informed and conscientious dispensing pharmacist are held in high estimation by those most conversant with his methods. A complete assortment of drugs, medicines and chemicals is constantly kept in stock and physicians' prescriptions are compounded in the most approved and painstaking manner at short notice and at moderate rates. Among the other articles dealt in may be mentioned stationery, toilet articles, confectionery, cigars, soda water, etc., and there is a well selected circulating library on the premises which affords an excellent opportunity to read the latest novels and other popular works at nominal expense. Low prices are quoted on all the goods handled.

J. E. Vollmer, House and Carriage Painter, Shop west of Common, South Framingham, Mass.—Of course "anybody can paint a house," So can anybody make a suit of clothes—after a fashion—but that fashion is apt to be much more striking than attractive. The fact is, in painting as in everything else, skill and experience are necessary in order to secure satisfactory results. It pays every time to have painting done by competent and responsible parties, and those who think to save a dollar by doing the work themselves or by entrusting it to somebody who knows no more than they do, may save *that* dollar but it will only be at the expense of many another in the long run. It does not cost a great deal to have painting properly done, and in this connection we may call attention to the facilities possessed by Mr. J. E. Vollmer, for he not only does work equal to the best but also quotes moderate rates on every order. Mr. Vollmer is prepared to do house and carriage painting of all descriptions and uses no inferior stock, as indeed may be judged from his reputation for turning out thoroughly dependable work. His shop is located west of the Common, and orders given in person or sent by mail will be given immediate and painstaking attention. Mr. Vollmer claims to have invented an embossing oil for restoring old paint (providing the paint is still there) to its original color, and warrants the same to last eight years and hold its luster. It is exclusively for outside work. *Sign work* of all descriptions is done on wood, glass or any substance, interior decorating, paper hanging in all its branches are promptly attended to at moderate rates. Wall and ceiling paper is carried in stock and sold at lowest market rates. Mr. Vollmer has done first-class jobs not only in Framingham but in the surrounding towns and gives by consent the following references : A. R. Newton & Son, Bridges & Co., F. E. Brooks, Old Colony House, B. F. Coburn, R. H. Nelson, W. H. Hastings of South Framingham, and Charles H. Tilton and Mrs. L. Adams, Ashland.

Charles L. Curtis, Ph.G., Pharmacist, opposite Odd Fellows Block, Hollis Street, South Framingham, Mass.—The pharmacy carried on by Charles L. Curtis, Ph G., stands high in the confidence of the public, for its proprietor is not only an educated and experienced dispensing chemist, but also an enterprising man of business, as is proved by the character and extent of the stock he offers and the uniformly low rates quoted on the articles constituting the same. Mr. Curtis was born in Stoneham, Mass., and has been identified with the drug business since 1876 and with his present undertaking since 1882. The premises made use of are located on Hollis street, opposite Odd Fellows Hall, and measure 20×45 feet. The assortment of drugs, medicines and chemicals is exceptionally complete in every department, and being obtained from the most reliable sources, may be depended upon in every respect. Mr. Curtis is prepared to compound physicians' prescriptions in the most accurate and satisfactory manner, having the latest improved facilities at his command and sparing no pains to ensure promptness as well as absolute correctness in the filling of such orders. No exorbitant charges are made, the rates quoted being as low as is consistent with the use of dependable ingredients. Toilet and fancy goods are dealt in to a considerable extent, as are also cigars, confectionery, etc. A specialty

is made of soda water trade, and probably there is no dealer in this vicinity who enjoys any more favorable reputation for furnishing the very best beverage in this line; instead of reducing prices and furnishing a correspondingly cheap drink, Mr. Curtis retains regular prices, and gives the public a quality of soda water that draws and holds an appreciative patronage which demands his fountain to run twelve months in the year, a fact that commends this branch of his business more than anything that might be said of it. Employment is given to two efficient and courteous assistants, and customers may safely depend upon receiving immediate and polite attention.

A. M. Lang, Dry Goods and Small Wares, Agent for Lewando's Dye House, under Elm wood Opera House, South Framingham.—Mr. A. M. Lang is well known to be one of the most energetic and successful business men carrying on operations in this vicinity, and the magnitude of the trade he has built up since assuming control of his present enterprise in 1884, shows that the residents of this section are not at all backward in appreciating honorable and pushing methods. Mr. Lang was born in Stratton, N. H., and owes much of his success to the careful and constant personal supervision given every detail of his business. His store has an area of 1200 square feet, and contains one of the most clean and desirable stocks of dry goods, small wares, etc., to be found in the county. Space forbids any detailed mention of it, but we may say in passing that it comprises full lines of staple goods together with the latest fashionable novelties the market affords. The prices are what tell the story nowadays, and those quoted by Mr. Lang prove his business abilities much more clearly than any words of ours could do. His customers have the satisfaction of knowing that they are getting strictly dependable goods at bottom figures, and no further assurance is needed to bring about a large and rapidly growing trade. This is the agency of Lewando's Dye House, and work sent here will be dyed in the very best style of the art at short notice and at moderate expense.

E. F. Hunt, Meat, Fruit and Provisions, Fine Fruits a specialty, Concord Street, South Framingham, Mass.—The difficulty met with by some housekeepers in obtaining uniformly satisfactory provisions, is in the majority of cases the result of carelessness for there are quite a number of dealers who take pains to furnish their customers with strictly reliable goods, and if a little care be exercised in the placing of orders the advantages gained will fully repay whatever trouble may be involved in so doing. Mr. E. F. Hunt is one of those who make it a point to handle only dependable goods, and as his prices are as satisfactory as the quality of the articles dealt in, he has built up an extensive business since beginning operations in 1879. Mr. Hunt was born in Sudbury, Mass., and served in the army during the late war. He is very generally known in this vicinity, and his establishment on Concord street is well patronized by those who appreciate enterprising and honorable business methods. Meats and provisions in general are always in stock, and a specialty is made of fine fruits, a full selection of these delicacies being offered to choose from at prices in strict accordance with the lowest market rates.

A. M. Eames & Co., manufacturers of Fine Carriage Wheels, South Framingham, Mass.— From the cross section of a log to the light, elegant carriage wheel of the present day is a long step, and yet even now in the countries to the south of us, notably Mexico, the large majority of the heavier teams have no better wheels than such as can be made by sawing a tolerably round log across. Of course it requires no little skill to make a wheel that shall combine lightness, strength and durability, and the operations necessary to accomplish this result are many and interesting, as may be seen by a visit to the establishment conducted by Messrs A. M. Eames & Co., in this town. Mr. A. M. Eames has associated with him in conducting the manufacturing, Mr. E. A. Eames, both of whom served in the army during the Rebellion, and both of whom are widely known in this vicinity. The business was founded in 1877, and a large wholesale and retail trade has been built up, their productions ranking second to none in the market. The premises made use of comprise a three-story shop measuring 40 × 50 feet, and an ell of the dimensions of 35 × 40 feet, with large three-story store house, 40 × 40, connected with factory by bridge. An extensive plant of improved machinery being run by a thirty-five-horse engine. Fine carriage wheels of all sizes are very largely manufactured, as well as wagon and cart wheels of superior quality, and the reputation of the firm for using the best of stock and allowing no poor work to leave the factory is too well known to require dwelling upon. Orders are filled at short notice, and the prices quoted will compare very favorably with those named by any dealer in equally dependable goods. Band and circular sawing and wood turning are done in the best manner to order, the charges made in this department of the business being uniformly moderate.

H. C. Bowers, Ladies' and Gents' Restaurant, Union Block, South Framingham.—Some persons have very curious ideas concerning what the public desire in a restaurant, and act as though they thought that gaudy furnishing, fancy crockery, etc., were of more importance than food. This is a mistake, most of us visit a restaurant because we are hungry, and although bright and cheerful surroundings are excellent in their way, still they will not make up for any lack of food, or for slowness and stupidity of service. Mr. H. C. Bowers appears to have struck about the correct combination in his restaurant in Union Block, Waverly street, and although he has only carried on the establishment since the beginning of the year 1889, he has already greatly increased its popularity. He was born in this town, and served three years in the army during the Rebellion. The restaurant has an area of 1250 square feet, without counting the cook-room, and employment is given to six assistants, the table girls being relatives of the proprietor, and prompt and courteous service is one of the distinguishing features of the management. The bill of fare is varied enough to suit everybody, the food is the best that the market affords and the cookery is first class in every respect. Mr. Bowers assumes that his guests are hungry when they visit him, and consequently looks out for quantity as well as for quality in catering to them. Very reasonable prices are quoted, and it is no wonder that "business is rushing" at this well-managed establishment.

H. L. Sawyer, Hardware, Furnaces, Stoves and Ranges, Tin, Copper, Sheet Iron Work, and Plumbing, South Framingham, Mass.—The business carried on by Mr. H. L. Sawyer was founded over a score of years ago and was for some time confined to the handling of stoves, tin ware, etc., but it has gradually developed in every department, and now embraces the sale of hardware in general as well as of all the goods originally dealt in. Mr. Sawyer is a native of Ashburnham, Mass., and is widely known in South Framingham and vicinity. The premises utilized are very spacious, comprising warerooms having an area of 2500 square feet and a two-story workshop fitted up with every facility for the doing of tin, copper, sheet-iron work and plumbing, at short notice and in a neat and durable manner. The stock of hardware is very complete, and the furnaces, ranges and stoves handled by Mr. Sawyer represent the latest and most improved productions in this line. He quotes manufacturers' prices on these goods, and intending purchasers would best serve their own interests by giving him a call. Employing twenty efficient assistants, he is prepared to fill the most extensive orders for sheet-iron work, plumbing, etc., without delay, and guarantees entire satisfaction to customers, as all work is done by skilled hands under careful supervision, and the results attained are sure to be fully up to expectations in every respect.

Clifford Folger & Co., Foreign and Domestic Dry Goods, Boots and Shoes, Concord and Howard Streets, South Framingham, Mass.—It is now about twelve years since Clifford Folger came to South Framingham and established the dry goods business of Clifford Folger & Co. in the building that was known at that time as the Richardson Straw Shop—having at that time as partners the concern for whom he had been working as a salesman—this state of affairs continued for one year when he bought out their interest and took as a partner W. H. Bourne who was working with him at that time—he remaining in the concern until 1884, when they jointly bought out a store in Milford—Mr. Bourne taking charge of that branch of the business—after about one year they dissolved partnership and Mr. Bourne took the Milford business and Mr. Folger remaining and assuming the entire control of the business in South Framingham. Since then Clifford Folger & Co. have started two branch stores, one in Franklin and one in Westboro, both of which are doing a good business—by running three stores they are enabled to buy goods in large quantities and by doing so can get low prices which they can afford to give their customers the advantage of. They carry a large stock of staple domestic and foreign dry goods, by far the largest stock between Boston and Worcester, consequently command a large trade. They have the confidence of their customers gained no doubt by fair dealing in the past—and by carrying only such goods as they are willing to guarantee, or if of a cheap grade they are represented and sold for just what they are. South Framingham has grown rapidly since they established their business here, but they have more than kept pace with the growth of the town. They occupy at the present time a store with floor room of about 5000 square feet with frontage on both Concord and Howard streets. They carry as large a stock and have as attractive a store as can be found in many of our larger cities.

———

H. S. Drake, Photographic Studio, Waverly Street, South Framingham, Mass.—Economical habits are, no doubt, most excellent things to have, but unless accompanied by a due amount of discretion they are apt to lead their possessor most wofully astray in certain contingencies. For example, that economy which causes a man to patronize a photographer who does inferior work and consequently is obliged to quote very low rates, is rather a cause of waste than of saving, for an inferior photograph is of little value and it is doubtless better to go without altogether than to ask your friends to accept pictures of you which are neither good likenesses nor attractive ornaments. Not that we would give the idea that it is necessary to pay an extravagant price in order to secure satisfactory results. The residents of South Framingham and vicinity know better than this, for many of them have patronized the studio carried on by Mr. H. S. Drake on Waverly street, and have thus learned that reasonable prices and the best of work are by no means inconsistent, for Mr. Drake has met with great success in producing life-like and finely finished portraits, and his rates are low enough to suit the most limited means. He is a native of Hartford, Vt., and served in the army three years, inaugurating his present enterprise in this town in 1883. Photography in all its branches is carried on by the aid of the most improved appliances, etc., orders are promptly filled and every caller may safely depend upon receiving immediate and courteous attention.

———

Winthrop House, J. H. Jordon, Proprietor. Special Rates to Commercial Travellers, South Framingham, Mass.—Probably every traveller has his own idea of what constitutes a perfectly managed hotel, but there are certain points on which all reasonable persons are agreed, and as these points are embodied in the management of the Winthrop House it is perfectly natural that this hotel should hold a high place in the favor of the travelling public. It has been carried on by the present proprietor, Mr. J. H. Jordon, since July, 1889, and the disposition shown by this gentleman to make his guests feel at home and to provide for all reasonable wants, has gained for him, even in this short time, great personal popularity among those who have experienced his hospitality. The Winthrop House can accommodate fifty guests, and is a well-arranged and comfortably furnished hotel which is maintained in the best of condition and is very conveniently located. The terms of the house are uniformly moderate, and as special rates are made for commercial travellers, this numerous and energetic fraternity make it a point to put up at the Winthrop whenever circumstances render it possible to do so. One can get more "inside" information from a company of commercial travellers regarding hotel accommodations in half an hour than could otherwise be obtained in a year, and that the comparisons made in such gatherings are by no means unfavorable to the Winthrop House, may be judged from its wide popularity among the "knights of the road." Mr. Jordon sets a good table, and employs seven competent and efficient assistants.

———

GEORGE RICE. M. D..

PHARMACIST,

NOBSCOT BLOCK,

SO. FRAMINGHAM, MASS.

Established 1872.

———

South Framingham Furniture Company.— Everybody must have furniture, everybody must have carpets, and everybody should have spring-beds, not to mention mattresses or feather beds, for these are very powerful aids in resting a tired body, and the body that works to earn the money to buy them should be made as comfortable as possible. The average individual spends one-third of his life in bed, and therefore it is important that the latter be made as healthful and easy as is consistent with circumstances. Should any of our readers have occasion to purchase any of the articles mentioned we can recommend to them a first class establishment at which to buy, for that conducted by the South Framingham Furniture Company will be found to fully merit this description. Not only as regards the quality of the many articles handled, but also by reason of the exceptionally low figures quoted on the same. In buying furniture it is always well to remember that durability is at least as important as appearance, and the only way to get durable as well as handsome goods is to patronize a dealer who not only guarantees his articles to prove as represented but whose guarantee is worth something. No one can successfully deny that this company "fills the bill" in both these respects.

SAXONVILLE.

D. E. Thompson, dealer in Watches, Clocks and Jewelry; Repairing in all its Branches, Engraving in Any Style; Jewelry Made to Order, Saxonville, Mass.—The time was (and not so very long ago either), when a man of modest means hesitated about buying a watch even when he had the money to purchase one, for fear of the expense attendant upon keeping it in running order. But the charges for watch repairing, cleaning, etc., have been greatly reduced within the last few years, and it is now possible for everybody to "support a watch" as the saying is, who has occasion to use one. We are pleased to call your attention to the business conducted by Mr. D. E. Thompson, dealer in watches, clocks and jewelry. He makes a specialty of repairing watches, clocks or jewelry in all its branches, and all who have had work done here can testify to its thoroughness and to the moderate price charged for the same. The premises are located in Odd Fellows Block, Saxonville, and will measure 20×30 feet. Mr. Thompson also has a show case in the post office where he has a fine display of choice articles in his line of trade. Mr. Thompson is a native of Saxonville, Mass., and has been engaged in this business since 1885, and has many friends in this town. He gives his personal attention to engraving in all styles, as well as to jewelry, which he will make to order. He has a competent assistant and all customers are treated politely, and satisfaction is warranted to all who may leave their orders or purchase goods at this store.

M. A. McGrath, dealer in Hats, Caps and Gents' Furnishings, Clothing, etc., also Undertakers, Saxonville, Mass.—It is not always the most imposing appearing establishments that are the most reliable and worthy of patronage, and, in many cases, it will be found that more dependence can be placed in the announcements issued by those carrying on comparatively small enterprises than in those coming from the proprietors of more prominent undertakings. The reason for this state of affairs is that the proprietor of the smaller store will strive to get and to keep your individual custom, while the other will depend more upon the transient trade, and caters chiefly to that. Mr. M. A. McGrath commenced business here in 1882, and has built up a good, steadily increasing trade and patronage by showing the people that it would be to their advantage to purchase of him. Mr. McGrath is a native of Saxonville. One floor is occupied which measures 450 feet, and a well selected assortment of hats, caps, gents' furnishings and ready-made clothing is always to be found on hand. These goods are all warranted to prove as represented, and the proprietor's experience is valuable in knowing what goods will best please his customers, and from his personal acquaintance with them he can select such materials as they are most likely to desire. Mr. McGrath is also undertaker and keeps on hand such articles as are demanded in this branch of his business, such as coffins, robes, etc. He gives general satisfaction in every department that may require his services.

Mrs. A. H. Danforth, dealer in Foreign and Domestic Dry Goods, Millinery, Fancy Goods, Sewing Machine Needles, etc. Agency for Mme. Demorest's Reliable Patterns, Saxonville, Mass.—Among the most popular retail dealers in foreign and domestic dry goods and millinery in this vicinity deserving special mention is Mrs. A. H. Danforth, who has been engaged in this business for about 40 years, and is recognized in the trade as one of the most honorable, fair dealing and accomplished business women of Saxonville, Mass. She is a native of this town and well known to a large circle of friends. Her store is well located and covers a space of 900 square feet, and is plentifully stocked with all the novelties as well as the staples in this line of trade. A full line of millinery goods is carried, which is well selected and of the newest styles and designs. Special attention is given to order work, and customers may be assured that their individual tastes will be consulted and every effort made to give entire satisfaction. Fancy goods in a large variety may always be found, also sewing machine needles, etc. Mrs. Danforth is agent for Mme. Demorest's reliable patterns. She exhibits the best of taste and judgment in the selection of her assortment of goods, and this house has gained a place second to none in the retail trade of this neighborhood. Two competent and reliable assistants are employed, and all who patronize this store will be promptly attended to.

D. O. Frost, dealer in Furnaces, Ranges, Britannia, Wooden, Plated and Hard Ware; Wood, Copper and Iron Pumps; Sheet Lead, Sheet Zinc; Lead and Akron Drain Pipe; Lamp Goods, Brooms, Brushes, etc. Job work solicited. Saxonville, Mass.—It would greatly surprise many persons who pride themselves on their economy, to learn that they were throwing away money every day, but this is by no means an unusual practice, for it is just those who are over saving that will persist in using an old style or worn out furnace or range, and consequently consume enough extra fuel in the course of a year or so, to buy a range or furnace of the latest and most improved kind. To get an idea of the remarkable improvements which have lately been made in such articles, visit the establishment conducted by Mr. D. O. Frost in Saxonville, and examine his stock of furnaces and ranges, for it is made up of the latest inventions in this line, and is well worthy of inspection, and all desired information will be cheerfully given on application. This enterprise has been conducted by different members of the Frost family for fifty years, and the present proprietor, Mr. D. O. Frost, has had control since 1874. This gentleman is a native of Saxonville. The premises utilized consist of one floor measuring 25×80 feet, and a basement, and contain in addition to the goods before mentioned, a full assortment of britannia, wooden, plated and hardware; wood, copper and iron pumps; sheet lead, sheet zinc; lead and Akron drain pipe; lamp goods, brooms, brushes, etc. Job work is solicited, and it will be done in the most workmanlike manner, and the charges made are uniformly moderate. Employment is given to a capable assistant, and every customer will be treated in a satisfactory manner.

HISTORICAL SKETCH

OF

NATICK, MASS.

Natick is one of the very few Massachusetts towns whose names are of Indian origin, and certainly it is peculiarly fitting that the aboriginal origin of Natick should be thus indicated, for there is not a town in the State, or indeed in all New England, whose early history is more intimately identified with the first inhabitants of this country. For many years this territory was the home of Eliot's "Praying" Indians, and even at this late day the spade or the plow frequently brings to light relics of the comparatively advanced stage of civilization which these so-called "savages" had attained. They came to have a genuine affection for the fields on which they worked faithfully and persistently; and the unfounded jealousy and baseless mistrust which finally caused the authorities to banish them from the territory they had improved, not only severely tried their loyalty to the whites but greatly intensified the general distrust of English promises which has for centuries complicated the "Indian question." Yet these Praying Indians, although forced to abandon Natick and take up their abode on Deer Island, Boston Harbor, kept their promise to Eliot, and assisted the whites to repel the attacks of hostile tribes and rendered invaluable assistance in learning of the plans of the enemy, and warning exposed settlements of proposed raids.

Those at all familiar with the early history of New England are acquainted with the facts bearing upon John Eliot's missionary labors at Nonantum, and therefore we need not make extended reference to them, it being necessary only to state that the first settlement of Natick was brought about by Eliot's desire to remove his converts to a point where they would not suffer from the influence of the whites. He had some difficulty in finding a suitable site for his proposed settlement, but finally acted upon the advice of one of his converts and chose what was afterwards to be known as Natick.

The influence he had gained over the Indians is evidenced by what he writes concerning the first action taken to improve the territory: "When the grass was fit to cut, I sent some Indians to mow, and others to make hay, because we must oft ride hither in the autumn, and in the spring before any grass is come, and there is provision for our horses. Their work was performed well, as I found when I went up to them with my man to order it."

The natural and acquired distaste and disdain of the Indian warrior for physical labor, aside from that connected with war and hunting, has often been cited to show why permanent Indian civilization is impossible, but Eliot could induce his converts to work, even when they were not under his supervision, and the entire history of his labors with the Indians furnishes an unanswerable argument in favor of their capacity to become good citizens if properly treated and intelligently encouraged.

CLARK'S BLOCK, WEST SIDE MAIN STREET, NATICK.

One of the first public works carried out at the new settlement was the building of a foot-bridge, eighty feet in length, across the Charles River, and a few houses also were built, but wigwams were generally preferred to these, they being warmer and far more portable. A large fort was soon constructed, and in 1651 a frame-building measuring 50 × 25 feet was erected, the lower story being used for church and school purposes, and the upper floor for the storage of furs and other valuables. The frames and boarding were all sawed out by the Indians, the help of an English carpenter being given at the raising only. October 8, 1651 was signalized by a visit from Governor Endicott and other prominent men, and a sermon was preached by one of the Indians and another by Eliot. All the converts joined in singing a psalm and according to the governor they were "pretty tunable" in their delivery.

The chief men of the village consulted with him about a grist mill they proposed to build, and showed such enterprise and ability that Endicott afterward expressed himself as being "astonished and delighted" with what he learned that day. Natick became a prominent missionary centre and many teachers and preachers were trained here to extend the Gospel throughout New England. After the breaking out of King Philip's war in 1675, many of the whites became distrustful of the Christian Indians, who finally were ordered by the General Court to confine themselves to five villages, of which Natick was one, and not to go more than a mile from either of these communities. But even this restriction did not

EAST SIDE OF MAIN STREET, NATICK.

sufficiently reassure the alarmed ones, and the Indians of Natick were banished to Deer Island, being driven there at half an hour's notice and forced to abandon the great bulk of their property. Although some of the Indian families returned to Natick after the war, and their rights of ownership were admitted, the exile to Deer Island ended the town's prosperity as an Indian settlement, and the death of Eliot aided to discourage the original proprietors from asserting their rights. The white population steadily increased, and January 3, 1745, Natick plantation became a precinct by legislative act, and the Indians lost their citizenship and could not sell their own land without the permission of the General Court. In 1749 a census was taken and it was found there were 166 Indians then in Natick—men, women and children,—the most of whom lived on Pegan Plain.

Both the white and the Indian residents were well represented in the French and Indian war and the military training then received had its effect in after years, for the town was prompt in organizing "minute men" to resist English tyranny, and sent a company to embarrass the retreat of the British, April 19, 1775. The enthusiasm which permeated the community may be judged from the fact that in one case where a recruit needed a suit of clothes, the sheep were sheared, the material made and the garments completed by twelve maidens in twenty-four hours —a wonderful achievement in those days. A large proportion of the inhabitants enlisted and the town was represented on many bloody and famous fields.

Natick was incorporated in 1781, and nearly twenty years after that date, or in 1800, its population was only 694. Being then a farming community its growth was slow, and in 1830 there were but 890 persons in town. From 1830 to 1850 the population increased by leaps and bounds, for shoe manufacturing was then rapidly and constantly extending, and it seemed as though the industry would never cease its almost phenomenal development. The population showed a gain of forty-four per cent. from 1830 to 1840, as compared with five per cent. from 1820 to 1830, and from 1840 to 1850 the population doubled, and nearly doubled again in the succeeding decade.

The opening of the railroad in 1835, greatly aided the growth of the centre, which was afterward known as Natick, the older village taking the name of South Natick. The remaining village—Felchville—is so-named from Natick's original shoe manufacturer, Asa Felch, who first made sale shoes in 1827. For some years his workshop was a room in his house, and he kept no books for a long time. finding it easy to keep account of his transactions "in his head." Mr. Felch manufactured brogans, and the business is still in successful operation, although its founder died about twelve years ago. Henry Wilson came to Natick and went to work shoemaking in December, 1833, becoming an employer five years later. He was chosen United States' Senator in 1855, and as the friend and colleague of Charles Sumner he rendered most efficient service during the troublous times preceding the Rebellion. Mr. Wilson died, November 22, 1875, while holding the position of vice-president, and the "Natick cobbler," has left a name behind him which proves that public ability and private virtues are sometimes very prominently combined in one man.

Natick's schools have always been liberally supported, and will now compare favorably with those of any community in the State, of no greater population. The educational advantages of the town are materially increased by the existence of excellent public libraries, which are very generally patronized.

Natick has suffered severely at times from fire but the lesson has not been thrown away, there being a finely organized and well-equipped fire department capable of coping with any emergency liable to arise. The water works are ample and well-maintained, and the town offers many advantages to enterprising manufacturers, and to merchants as well, for the local trade is not only already extensive but is steadily increasing, and the conditions are such that outside competition can easily be met.

LEADING BUSINESS MEN

OF

NATICK.

O. H. Burleigh, Fire and Life Insurance Agency, Odd Fellows' Block, corner Main and Pond Streets, Natick.—The general insurance agency conducted by Mr. O. H. Burleigh, was established in 1815 by Mr. E. P. Hollis and is one of the best known enterprises of the kind in this section of the State. The present proprietor is a native of this town and has had eighteen years' experience in this line of business and been identified with the enterprise in question for more than ten years, during which time the business has very largely developed. Mr. Burleigh's main office is at No. 44 Kilby street, room 10, Boston, where he may be found from 11 to 1 o'clock ; his office in Natick being open day and evening. He is prepared to place insurance in any company authorized to do business in Massachusetts, and is the regular accredited agent for the following representative organizations, among which will be noticed six of the strongest mutual companies in the State : Home, New York, N. Y.; Insurance Co. of North America, Philadelphia, Pa ; Lancashire, Manchester, Eng.; Phœnix, London, Eng.; Niagara, New York, N. Y.; Hartford, Hartford, Conn.; Fire Association, Philadelphia, Pa.; Fire Association, London, Eng.; American, New York, N. Y.; Citizens, Pittsburgh, Pa.; Traders and Mechanics, Lowell, Mass.; Merchants and Farmers, Worcester, Mass.; Dorchester, Neponset, Mass.; Quincy, Quincy, Mass.; Middlesex, Concord, Mass.; Holyoke, Salem, Mass. Life, accident, plate-glass and steam-boiler insurance will also be procured at short notice, and insurance of all kinds will be effected at the lowest rates consistent with absolute security. Mr. Burleigh issues a circular giving a few practical hints to insurers which are the outcome of years of experience and are worthy of careful consideration. He is prepared to buy and sell real estate on commission, negotiate mortgages, collect rents and secure loans on personal property, besides being agent for prominent western mortgage and loan associations. Mr. Burleigh is a notary public and justice of the peace. As may be imagined, Mr. Burleigh is a very busy man but he gives prompt and painstaking attention to every communication and is always ready to cheerfully give any desired information concerning matters coming within the scope of his operations.

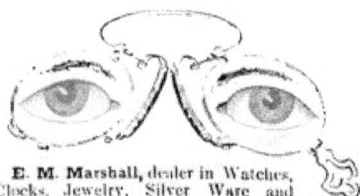

familiar with their present line of business and give it such close and painstaking personal attention as to assure having the service kept at the very highest standard of efficiency. The lowest market rates are quoted on all the commodities dealt in, and every article sold is guaranteed to prove precisely as represented.

E. M. Marshall, dealer in Watches, Clocks, Jewelry, Silver Ware and Optical Goods, Fine Watch Repairing. Store of the Standard Time, No. 3 Clark's Block, Natick, Mass.—There is certainly no good reason why practically everybody should not be provided with an accurate time-keeper nowadays, for both watches and clocks have been greatly improved of late years and at the same time the cost of them has been very materially reduced. "Time is money," as every school-boy knows, and however careless we may be of our own time we have no right to waste that of other people by being late in meeting engagements, etc., so that a reliable time-piece is a necessity as well as a convenience. As good a place as we know of at which to purchase anything in this line is at the store conducted by Mr. E. M. Marshall at No. 3 Clark's Block, for here may be found a varied and very carefully chosen stock and the prices are always as low as the lowest. Mr. Marshall was born in Nantucket, Mass., and served more than three years in the army during the Rebellion, holding a commission as first lieutenant and quartermaster, when mustered out. He inaugurated his present enterprise in 1875 and has developed it by giving careful personal attention to the wants of customers and sparing no pains to give full value for money received in every instance. Watches, clocks, jewelry, silver-ware and optical goods are extensively dealt in, bottom prices being quoted and every article being fully guaranteed to prove as represented. Particular attention is paid to fine watch repairing and orders will be filled at very short notice. Mr. Marshall has had long and constant experience in the delicate art of testing eye sight and fitting lenses to the eyes. Besides having had a thorough course of instruction with Prof. Cushman of New York, he has a fine and costly set of *test lenses* and other appliances by which the slightest error in eye sight can be detected and corrected. No charge is made for examination.

Dodson & Springer, dealers in Pure Family Lard, Oxford Sausages, etc., Natick, Mass.— The enterprise conducted by Messrs. Dodson & Springer is in some respects unique, for although there is no lack of dealers in meats and provisions in this vicinity, there is no other concern making a leading specialty of pure family lard and Oxford sausages. That the public approve of the methods of this firm is proved by the fact that an extensive patronage has already been attained, although operations were not begun until 1889. The premises utilized have an area of about 1,500 square feet and are exceptionally well stocked, for the firm do both a wholesale and retail business and make it a point to be ready to fill all orders without delay. The partners are Messrs. A. S. Dodson and F. W. Springer, the former being a native of England and the latter of Canada. Both are thoroughly

Fiske & Co., Paints, Oils, Varnishes, Brushes, Glass and Sporting Goods; Hardware, Doors, Sash and Blinds, Furnaces, Stoves and Tinware, Plumbing. Steam and Water Piping, Fiske Block, South Avenue, Natick, Mass.—Natick is regarded as an excellent place in which to do business by wide awake men fully "up to the times," in every respect, but even in this town but few enterprises can be pointed out which have developed so rapidly of late years as has that now conducted by Messrs. Fiske & Co. Operations were begun a number of years ago, and the ownership has changed several times, the firm of Sargent & Heaton being succeeded by Messrs. Heaton & Co., who gave place to the present proprietors in 1888. Mr. J. M. Fiske is a native of this town, while both his associates, Messrs. C. H. Turner and G. L. Hill, were born in Maine. The firm utilize spacious and well-arranged premises located in Fiske Block, South Avenue, they comprising three floors and a basement of the dimensions of 49 × 70 feet. An immense stock is constantly carried, and some idea of its variety may be gained from the fact that it includes hardware, paints, oils, varnishes, brushes and glass; sporting goods, doors, sash and blinds, furnaces, stoves and tin ware, besides other commodities of equal importance. Messrs. Fiske & Co., do both a wholesale and retail business and are prepared to furnish anything in their line at short notice and at positively bottom prices. Estimates and orders for plumbing, steam and hot-water heating and gas piping are assured immediate and painstaking attention, employment being given to twelve efficient assistants, and all work being fully warranted in every respect.

Beal's Clothing House, dealers in Men's, Boys' and Children's Clothing, Hats, Caps and Furnishing Goods, Masonic Block, Six Doors South of Post-office, Natick, Mass.—Clothing is generally divided into two classes—custom-made and ready-made—but many people apparently fail to realize that there are numerous sub-divisions in these classes, and as a consequence expose themselves to the chance of imposition. First class ready-made clothing is for all practical purposes fully the equal of that made to order, while it is obtainable at a much lower figure, and it is so far superior to the "cheap" tailoring now so common in the market that comparison is almost out of the question. "Beal's Clothing House," and dependable clothing are very intimately associated in the minds of our Natick readers, and it is very natural that such should be the case, for the establishment to which we refer has been carried on by the present proprietor for more than ten years, and has been conducted on straightforward principles from the very beginning, full value for money received being one of the most prominent guiding rules of the management. The owner is Mr. Leander Beal of the well-known Boston house of Miner, Beal & Co., and the enterprise is under the management of Mr. Geo. Healy. The store is located in Masonic Block, six doors south of the post-office, and is 70 × 25 feet in dimensions, all available space being utilized in the accommodation of the large and complete stock which comprises men's, boys' and children's clothing of all descriptions. Hats, caps and furnishing goods are also well represented, the latest novelties being offered and bottom prices being quoted in every department of the business. Employment is given to three assistants, and callers may safely depend upon receiving prompt and courteous attention.

Pratt & Underwood, Boots, Shoes and Rubbers, No. 3 Clark's Block, Natick—This establishment was well known to the residents of Natick and vicinity in connection with the sale of boots, shoes and rubbers, before Messrs. Pratt & Underwood assumed control of the business in 1889, it having been inaugurated in 1875 by Mr. W. L. Doane, but the present firm offer still greater attractions in the line of footwear, and make a specialty of school shoes, every pair of which is warranted. A finely equipped store is occupied at No. 3 Clark's Block, measuring about 800 feet, and contains a heavy, varied and very skillfully chosen stock of new and desirable goods that cannot fail to satisfy the most fastidious. Mr. John H. Pratt and Mr. J. H. Underwood are both natives of Natick, and are extremely well known in this vicinity and giving close personal attention to the wants of customers. The stock of boots, shoes and rubbers is made up of the productions of the most reputable manufacturers and includes goods suited to all conditions of wear. The assortment of sizes is so complete that all feet can be fitted, while the patterns offered are almost endless in variety and comprise the latest novelties in foot-wear for both sexes. Well-made and fashionable boots and shoes of all kinds may always be had here at bottom prices, and every article is sold under a guarantee that it will prove just as represented.

The Natick Five Cents Savings Bank, Rooms 35 and 36 Clark's Block, Natick.—Countless sermons have been preached and numberless essays written on the advantages of economy and the desirability of acquiring saving habits, but there is a more powerful influence exerted by one such enterprise as the Natick Five Cents Savings Bank than by enough economic essays to completely fill this volume. One of the wisest sayings we have is "Example is better than precept," and even the most careless cannot fail to be impressed to some degree at least by the example of their neighbors whom they see putting money away week by week, month by month and year by year, until a firm barrier has been raised between them and that adversity which may visit any of us, and which as reasoning creatures we are bound to provide against by such means as are at our command. There is a secondary advantage gained by the formation of saving habits which is too often lost sight of, and that is the possession of a contented mind, for he who is doing his best as an intelligent man to guard his family against want cannot help becoming a better man for it in every way, and cannot help having more self respect than is possible for one who is acting irrationally and knows it, however he may try to hide the fact from himself. Of course the Natick Five Cents Savings Bank greatly encourages the amassing of small savings, for it receives deposits from 5 cents to $1,000, has invariably paid as high a rate of interest as consistent with the soundest banking policy, and during its more than thirty years of usefulness has so ably discharged its functions as to have gained the entire confidence of the community. The men identified with this bank are very widely and favorably known in general business as well as in financial circles, and the following list of officers will go farther than the most flattering list of assets could to establish the absolute solvency and reliability of the enterprise in the minds of Natick people: John O. Wilson, president; Leonard Winch, John L. Woodman, vice-presidents; Trustees, John O. Wilson, J. L. Woodman, Edward Clark, Francis Bigelow, F. H. Hayes, F. M. Boardman, F. E. Cummings, Leonard Winch, Riley Pebbles, G. W. Howe, E. P. Hollis, William Nutt, O. A. Felch, J. M. Forbush. Investing committee, Leonard Winch, William Nutt, Francis Bigelow, J. L. Woodman, F. H. Hayes, F. O. Baston. Treasurer, Frederick O. Baston. Operations were begun in 1859 and the amount now held on deposit exceeds $1,000,000. Deposits draw interest from the first days of February, May, August and November, and dividends are payable on the second Tuesday in May and November. Rooms 35 and 36 Clark's Block have been recently fitted up in a most convenient and attractive manner. A fine fire-proof vault and a massive burglar proof safe with time-lock attachment, are the effective agencies employed to protect the accounts of the bank. The bank hours are from 9 A. M. to 3 P. M.; deposits being received and payments made with very little delay or "red tape" of any kind.

Barnicle & Allen, Cash Grocers, West Central Street, Natick, Mass.—There is no line of business but what profits by the personal attention of the proprietors, but we question if there is any other department of trade in which the necessity of such personal supervision is more marked than is the case in the retail grocery business. The vast amount of petty detail it involves is one reason for this condition of affairs, for if such detail be not intelligently looked after an inefficient service must inevitably result. One of the best-managed, as it is one of the most popular, grocery stores located in this section is that conducted by Messrs. Barnicle & Allen on West Central street, and the main secret of the excellent management evident is the personal attention given the direction of affairs by the owners. Both P. H. Barnicle and J. H. Allen are Natick men by birth and are widely and favorably known in social and business circles. They started their present enterprise in 1887 and have worked hard and intelligently to build up their trade, employing strictly legitimate methods and sparing no pains to fully satisfy every reasonable customer. The store has an area of some 1200 square feet, and contains an exceptionally complete stock, comprising staple and fancy groceries, flour, grain, woodenware, etc., the goods being selected expressly for family trade and being in every instance guaranteed to prove just as represented. The firm quote bottom prices on all the commodities they handle, and employ two competent assistants, thus being in a position to assure prompt and careful attention to every caller.

F. E. Hooker, successor to James Adams, Funeral and Furnishing Undertaker and Auctioneer, connected by telephone, Adams' Block, Natick, Mass.—Although good sense forbids there being too much stress put on the thought of death under ordinary circumstances, still it is but the part of common prudence to be prepared to act with promptness and decision in any emergency, and therefore we feel that the information we propose to supply regarding the establishment now conducted by Mr. Frank E. Hooker in Adams' Block, Natick, Mass., will be neither out of place nor neglected. The establishment in question was founded over eighteen years ago. Mr. F. E. Hooker, the present proprietor, is fully prepared to assume entire control of funerals and to supply everything required at equitable rates, and all branches of the undertaking profession are carried on in a strictly first class manner. The premises occupied comprise two floors each 20 × 60 feet in dimensions, and are appropriately fitted up for the purposes for which they are used. Mr. Hooker has for fifteen years been an auctioneer and contemplates conducting a regular weekly auction sale room in connection with his present business. Mr. Hooker is a native of Sherborn, Mass., and is very well known and highly esteemed in Natick and vicinity. He was brought up in the business, his father and grandfather being undertakers before him, and having kept up with the times by attending schools for instruction in the art of embalming and care of the cadaver, and has had much practical experience, we therefore advise all in need of the services of a reliable undertaker to communicate with Mr. Hooker, as all orders, by telephone, or otherwise delivered, will receive prompt and courteous attention, and be executed in a most satisfactory manner.

DR. M. O. NELSON.

DENTIST.

Room 4,
Walcott Building.   Natick, Mass.

Cochituate House, Mrs. George F. Rogers, Proprietor, Board by the Day or Week. Particular attention Paid to Commercial Travelers. Main Street, Natick, Mass.—Since Mr. George F. Rogers assumed control of the Cochituate House, in 1883, it steadily gained in popularity, and commercial travelers will be glad to learn that the policy of paying particular attention to their interests, so successfully inaugurated by Mr. Rogers, is still continued by Mrs. Rogers, who has been in charge of the house since 1889. The Cochituate House is very centrally located, on Main street, and is a roomy and well-arranged structure capable of accommodating some thirty or forty guests. The premises are kept in first-class condition at all times, comparing very favorably in this respect with many large city hotels making very high pretensions, and no trouble is spared to make guests feel thoroughly at home, so that those who appreciate genuine comfort would do well to make it a point to put up at the Cochituate when business or pleasure calls them to this part of the State. Both regular and transient boarders will be accommodated and the bill of fare is certainly varied enough to suit all varieties of taste, while the food is abundant in quantity and is cooked in regular home style. Mrs. Rogers is uniformly moderate in her charges and evidently is determined to give her guests no reasonable cause for dissatisfaction. Such a policy cannot be too highly commended, and we take pleasure in heartily and unreservedly recommending the Cochituate House to our readers.

The Natick National Bank, Main Street, Corner of Summer Street, Natick, Mass.—Since the organization of the Natick National Bank in 1872, it has rendered constant and powerful aid in developing the best interests of this section, but valuable as this assistance has been in the past, it is but an earnest of what may be expected in the future if the bank but receive the hearty co operation which in view of its record it has a right to expect. It cannot be too strongly insisted upon that any business enterprise, and particularly a financial institution, is directly dependent upon the public for its facilities to offer first-class service, and the more generally those facilities are availed of the more largely can the capacity for usefulness be extended. The Natick National Bank transacts a general banking business on liberal principles; no charge being made on collections on New England, New York, New Jersey and the cities of Philadelphia, Baltimore and Washington; while foreign collections will be made at the lowest rates consistent with sound banking. United States bonds will be bought and sold without expense; and the accounts of banks, bankers, corporations, manufacturers, firms and individuals will be received on favorable terms. In this connection, the following statement of the condition of the bank at the close of business, October 11, 1889, will prove of interest; compared as it is with the condition of the institution three years ago:

RESOURCES.

	Oct. 11, 1886.	Oct. 11, 1889.
Loans and Discounts. . .	$227,551.08	$284,319.29
Furniture and Fixtures.	1,803.51	800.00
Real Estate, ...	1,070.87	
United States Bonds to secure Circulation,	100,000.00	50,000.00
Expense Account.	351.83	76.02
5 per cent. Redemption Fund.	2,450.00	2,250.00
Due from other National Banks	122.50	1 000.00
Stocks, Bonds and Mortgages, ...	15,450.00	15,250.00
North National Bank.	50,947.32	43,653.49
Cash on hand	19,056.49	28,963.72
	$418,803.60	$425,692.52

LIABILITIES.

	Oct. 11, 1886.	Oct. 11, 1889.
Capital Stock.	$100,000.00	$100,000.00
Surplus Fund.	20,000.00	25,000.00
Undivided Profits.	5,767.00	7,765.95
Circulation	90,000.00	45,000.00
Deposits.	202,064.60	247,926.57
Dividend Unpaid.	972.00	
	$418,803.60	$425,692.52

Those who contemplate opening a new account or changing their present banking correspondent may find it for their advantage to form a connection with this bank, and at all events may feel assured that any communication they may make will receive immediate and careful attention, while a personal conference with the bank officers may be had at any time. These gentlemen need no introduction to our Natick readers for they are all prominently identified with local interests, and their operations are of a nature which has made them widely known in general business circles. The president is Mr L. Winch,

the cashier, Mr. S. W. Holmes, and the board of directors Messrs. Harrison Harwood, Leonard Winch, Riley Pebbles, Edward Clark, O. A. Felch and Frank H. Hayes.

J. B. Moyse, dealer in Harnesses, Saddles, Whips, etc., 11 Wood's Block, South Ave., Natick, Mass. —No harness can combine strength and beauty unless it be carefully made from selected material, and most of the so called "cheap" harness are cheap only as regards first cost, the expense of keeping them in condition soon more than making up the difference in price between them and a really good article. Mr. J. B. Moyse, doing business at No. 11 Wood's Block, South avenue, Natick, Mass., carries a fine assortment of harnesses of all descriptions and quotes some very low prices, considering the quality of the goods offered. He has carried on his present enterprise since 1888, and has built up an extensive trade by supplying reliable articles at fair rates. The stock on hand includes heavy and light, single and double harness, and horse furnishings of all kinds. Mr. Moyse is a native of England, and is very well known throughout Natick. He is a practical harness maker, and is prepared to do such work to order at very short notice and at moderate rates. Harnesses will be oiled and repaired without delay, and as only skilled help is employed, Mr. Moyse is prepared to guarantee that all work done at his establishment will give complete satisfaction.

Moran & Buckley, dealers in Boots, Shoes, Slippers and Rubber Goods, Walcott Block, Natick, Mass.—We all have our own ideas on the subject of foot-wear, and there is but one way to successfully cater to all classes of trade and that is to carry a large and varied stock so that all tastes can surely be suited. The extensive business built up by Messrs. Moran & Buckley since they began operations in 1884 is due in great measure to the enterprise displayed in offering a full selection of the latest fashionable novelties to choose from, although the lowness of the prices quoted must also be given due credit, as must the policy of offering uniformly courteous attention to every caller. The firm is made up of Messrs. B. F. Moran and C. E. Buckley, both of whom are natives of this town. They give careful personal attention to the business, although employment is given to from one to three assistants, and no trouble is spared to assure immediate and satisfactory service to every customer. The premises utilized are located in Walcott Block, and are of the dimensions of 20x45 feet, every facility being at hand to enable operations to be carried on to the best possible advantage, including repairing in all its branches. The firm manufacture some of the goods they handle, and are in a position not only to quote absolutely bottom prices but to fully guarantee that every article sold shall prove precisely as represented.

Frank E. Houghton, Boarding, Baiting and Livery Stable Horses, Carriages, etc., Bought and Sold or Exchanged, opposite depot, Natick, Mass—When Mr. Frank E. Houghton founded his present business in 1875, he had just one horse, and those who know how well equipped his stable is to day need not be told that his business has developed wonderfully in every department. And yet, wonderfully is not quite the proper word to use in this connection, for the development referred to has been so earnestly worked for and is so thoroughly deserved that it is certainly no wonder that it has been brought about. Mr. Houghton is a native of Natick and has a very large circle of friends throughout this vicinity. He gives close personal supervision to affairs and takes pride in maintaining the enviable reputation now long associated with his establishment. The stables are located opposite the depot and contain fifty stalls. The office, stables, carriage floors, etc., cover 16,730 feet of ground, besides the large storage capacity of second floors, affording ample opportunity for the carrying on of an extensive boarding and baiting as well as a livery business. Some thoroughly desirable teams are to be hired here at reasonable rates and orders can generally be filled at a moment's notice. Mr. Houghton keeps two public carriages at the depot, hacks Nos. 1 and 2, and is prepared to convey large or small parties to adjoining towns at a moderate charge. Horses carriages, etc., are bought, sold and exchanged and those wishing to do anything in this line would best serve their own interests by giving Mr. Houghton a call. The stable has telephone connections and all orders are assured immediate and painstaking attention.

People's Steam Laundry, D. A. Mahony, Proprietor, 7 and 9 Common Street, Natick, Mass.—It is proverbially difficult for doctors to agree, and when practically all physicians are agreed on a certain point the presumption is that there can be but little to say on the other side of the question. One point on which there is no dispute in the medical profession is the advisability of having all laundry work done outside the home. The doctors say that the steam and odor from the washing are apt to create and to spread disease, and they point out the fact that the process followed at a modern steam laundry totally destroys all disease germs which may exist in the clothing treated. The People's Steam Laundry is the first establishment of the kind to be opened in Natick and as it is equipped in first-class style throughout and is ably and progressively managed, there is ample reason for the great and growing popularity it has already attained. The proprietor, Mr. D. A. Mahony, served in the army and also in the United States' Navy, on the gun boat *Desota*, making over three years' service, and began operations in this town in 1886. The premises utilized by him are located at Nos. 7 and 9 Common street, and the facilities are sufficiently extensive to enable all work to be delivered promptly at the time promised. The charges are moderate and good work is guaranteed; all ladies' wear being handled exclusively by lady assistants and no precaution being neglected to ensure satisfaction to every reasonable customer. Mr. Mahony was three

years overseer of the poor and has been prominent in town affairs, especially on the temperance question, having been elected four or five times on the board of selectmen on the temperance question, his service as selectman is memorable on account of his refusal to sign licenses, the town having voted to grant them. Mr. Mahony carried the question to the Supreme Court and thus obtained a decision that he was not obliged to sign the licenses under the law as it thus stood.

Geo. C. Howe, Dry and Fancy Goods, Carpets and Furniture, Hogan's Block, Main Street, Natick, Mass.—One of the old established houses in this vicinity is that conducted by Mr. Geo. C. Howe. This flourishing business was founded by Mr. Howe in 1877 and has become a favorite resort for the residents of Natick when desiring anything in the dry goods or furniture line. The goods kept by this house are too well known throughout this section to need any especial remarks from us, suffice it to say it is the house at which to purchase dry goods of all kinds, including fancy goods, as well as carpets, of which he has a good assortment, such as extra supers, ingrains, hemp, straw matting and oilcloths. His is also the place to buy furniture, as he can offer many advantages to those who wish chamber sets, parlor suits, kitchen furniture, extension tables, centre tables, spring beds, mattresses, feathers, husks, mirrors, curtain fixtures, etc., etc. The premises occupied are located in Hogan's Block, Main street, and comprise two floors 20 × 60 feet each in dimensions. We commend this house to our readers as one whose reputation has been secured by a uniform system of fair and honorable dealing, which has ever characterized their transactions, as well as the excellent quality and reliability of all their goods.

E. A. Ring, dealer in Meats and Provisions, Wood's Block, Washington Street, Natick, Mass. Some few business men succeed by catering especially to one class of trade, but in the large majority of instances the only way to attain a large and permanent patronage is to spare no pains to satisfy the purchasing public in general, and it is just this policy intelligently and completely carried out which commends the enterprise conducted by Mr. E. A. Ring to the residents of Natick and vicinity, and which has already resulted in the building up of an extensive patronage although operations were not begun until 1889. Mr. Ring's store is located in Wood's Block, Washington street, and has an area of 1,000 square feet, so that ample opportunity is given to carry a large and varied stock, comprising meats and provisions of every description. As we have previously intimated, every class of trade is catered to, and whether a choice cut or piece of soup stock be wanted, whether your family is large small, delicate or robust, you can trade at this store to excellent advantage and have the satisfaction of knowing that you will be given full value for money paid in every instance. Mr. Ring employs three efficient assistants, and is consequently prepared to assure immediate and careful attention to all callers and to deliver orders at short notice.

Mitchell House, T. Mitchell, Proprietor, Natick.—Experienced travellers say that New England leads all other sections of the country as regards hotel accommodations, and that this superiority is not so manifest in the larger cities as in the smaller communities throughout the entire section. This judgment is gratifying of course to every thoroughbred Yankee and is probably correct, but if such be the case it argues ill for the comfort of travellers in other parts of the Union, for even here in New England the hotel accommodations are susceptible of great improvement. To be sure there are some thoroughly well-equipped and well managed public houses here, but these show all the more strongly the deficiencies of the others, and it is easy to see how one who puts up for any length of time at the Mitchell House will miss the luxuries and comforts there provided when he goes away. But of course that is no reason why they should not be availed of whenever possible, and we would certainly advise all who visit Natick for a long or short period to stop at the hotel in question, which is equipped with steam heat, electric lights and in short is first class in its appointments throughout. The premises are sufficiently capacious to accommodate forty guests, and the house is comfortably furnished and excellently well kept in every part. It was opened in 1888 by Mr. T. Mitchell, and has already secured a firm hold on the public favor, the patronage being extensive and constantly increasing. The table is in keeping with the other departments, being furnished with an abundance of palatable food at all seasons. The service is efficient and polite, and the terms of the house are uniformly moderate.

Samuel Emerson, manufacturer of Emerson's Soap Powder, Natick.—There are two ways in which dirt may be removed from the skin or from any fabric; the first being mechanically and by main force, the second chemically and by little or no force whatever. Many efforts have been made to devise a compound which would effectually dissolve and remove all dirt and grease without injuring the fabric treated, but up to the present time nothing has been found which will equal Emerson's Soap Powder, first put on the market in 1883. This is a sweeping claim but it can be proved to be well founded, and those who will use the soap powder in accordance with directions will find it to be not only the best but the most economical, as but a small quantity is required and the work of cleansing is done with marvellous ease. The inventor and patentee of this compound, Mr. Samuel Emerson, is a native of Charlestown, Mass., and is well-known in trade circles throughout Massachusetts, his powder being in active and increasing demand throughout the State. It is put up in one pound packages, and in order to protect the public from fraudulent imitations, the likeness and signature of the proprietor are on each package. Mr. Emerson manufactures the article himself and is prepared to furnish it in quantities to suit at very short notice. It is warranted positively harmless to the most delicate skin or fabric, and should be used in every family, both for laundry and toilet purposes.

Edward Clark, dealer in West India Goods, and Groceries, Crockery, Glass Ware, etc., Main Street, corner of Central, Natick, Mass.—A review of the leading business men of Natick which contained no mention of Mr. Edward Clark, might have some value as an oddity but could not by any stretch of the imagination be looked upon as complete, for this gentleman has long been a prominent figure in local affairs and has exerted a powerful influence in developing the best interests of the community. He is a native of Natick, holds the position of town treasurer, and is treasurer of the gas company, and a member of the board of directors of both the local banks. The West India and grocery store of which he is proprietor is the oldest establishment of the kind in town, and has been controlled for more than half a century by one family, Mr. Nathaniel Clark having commenced and continued it for about twenty five years, and the present owner for about thirty years. The premises made use of are located on Main street, corner of Central in Clark's Block, and comprise a main store of the dimensions of 24 × 70 feet, a grain and flour room 40 feet square, and three commodious basements. A very heavy stock is carried, made up of choice staple and fancy groceries, crockery ware, glass ware, etc., together with flour, feed, grain, etc. Despite the magnitude of the business orders can be filled at remarkably short notice, for employment is given to seven competent assistants and every facility is at hand to enable operations to be carried on to the best advantage. Mr. Clark quotes the lowest market rates on dependable goods and spares no pains to maintain the enviable reputation so long associated with this representative enterprise. Clark's Block in which this store is located, is the business block of the town and was built by Mr. Nathaniel Clark under the direction and management of his son, Mr. Edward Clark. It is a fine structure and a monument to the enterprise and public spirit which has marked the career of both father and son. Mr. Clark, senior, was for twenty years town treasurer and has three times been a member of the legislature.

Geo. W. Moulton, Agent, E. L. Moulton, Games, Toys, Confectionery and Fancy Goods, Washington Street, Natick, Mass.—This store is a very attractive place to visit, for the stock is varied enough to suit all tastes and is made up of articles that are worthy of careful examination and will bear comparison with any similar store in this section. The premises made use of contain about 800 square feet, and the assortment of goods on hand, includes games suitable for children of all ages, toys in great variety made to suit all purses and all times, and confectionery which may be found fresh and of good quality and variety. Mr. G. W. Moulton is a native of Natick. He served in the army for three years during the Rebellion, and is well and favorably known in this place. The line of holiday goods shown embraces about everything that can be thought of, we can only say that they must be seen to be appreciated, for their variety is almost endless, and they include the very latest novelties to be found in the market. All in want of birthday gifts or fancy goods will do well to pay a visit here.

F. J. Williams, Photographer, North Avenue, Natick, Mass.—It seems almost incredible that any person who had arrived at years of discretion should judge of the merits of an article entirely by its cost, but, nevertheless, it is undeniable that thousands of apparently intelligent people can be found who if shown two objects, similar in appearance but differing greatly in price, will deceive themselves into thinking that the higher priced one is immeasurably superior to the other. Some photographers take advantage of this peculiar human trait and quote exorbitant prices on work which is in no sense better than that which a discriminating buyer can obtain at a much smaller figure. Such, however, is not the policy pursued by Mr. F. J. Williams, or "Williams, the Photographer," as he is more generally known; and we have no hesitation in saying that those who wish to get absolutely first-class photographic work at absolutely bottom prices, cannot possibly do better than to call at the spacious and well equipped studio of the gentleman in question. It is located on North avenue and comprises two floors, measuring 25×37 feet, an entire building being occupied. The proprietor is a native of England, and founded the enterprise in 1880, removing to his present location in 1887. He gives close personal attention to the supervision of affairs and employs sufficient assistance to ensure the prompt filling of every order, photography in all its branches being extensively carried on and bottom prices being quoted in every department of the business.

George C. Wight, Salt and Fresh Provisions, Fruits and Vegetables. Summer Street, Natick, Mass.—Among the various dealers in meats and provisions doing business in Natick and vicinity, it would be impossible to find one better prepared to cater to all classes of trade than is Mr. George C. Wight, for in addition to carrying on a well stocked provision store on Summer street, he utilizes a slaughter house on Bacon street, where butchering is quite extensively engaged in. Mr. Wight's store was formerly known as the Natick Co-operative market, but has been under the control of the present proprietor since 1878. He was born in this town and has a very large circle of friends throughout this section. The store has an area of about 1,000 square feet and contains all necessary facilities for the storage and handling of the heavy and varied stock which comprises beef, mutton, lamb, veal, pork, lard, hams, sausages, and in short fresh, salted, smoked and pickled meats of all kinds, together with every variety of fruits and vegetables in the season. Eggs are also largely dealt in, these goods being received at frequent intervals and being of a quality that cannot fail to suit the most fastidious. Mr. Wight enjoys an extensive patronage, but callers are assured much prompter attention than is commonly given at smaller establishments, for five assistants are employed and all orders are filled without delay.

C. W. Burks, Undertaker, Furniture Dealer and Auctioneer, No. 10 South Avenue, Natick, Mass.—The business carried on by Mr. C. W. Burks at the above place of business is somewhat complex in character, for here will be found very commodious quarters where are displayed an assortment of new and second-hand furniture, sewing machines and findings, stoves, ranges, carpets, bedding, etc., in sufficient variety to meet the demand of the trade of this vicinity. Mr. Burks quotes prices as low as is consistent for honest goods. He is a public auctioneer and will attend to this line of business on satisfactory terms. The undertaking branch of the business is an important one, for a good line of caskets, robes, and undertakers sundries are kept in stock so that orders can be promptly filled, and the services of Mr. Burks as funeral director when desired can be had, thus relieving friends of all the care and anxious details incident to the burial of friends. Mr. Burks has had over twelve years experience having succeeded Mr. A. W. Burks in 1877, and hence is well known in this vicinity. His place of business is very convenient in location being but a few steps from the depot on South avenue.

Charles H. Morse, Agent, Prescription Druggist and Registered Pharmacist, Downs' Block, South Main Street, Natick, Mass.—One of the best equipped and most carefully managed prescription drug stores of which we have knowledge is that conducted by Mr. Charles H. Morse in Downs' Block, Main street, and those who have done business with this gentleman during the thirteen years that he conducted a similar establishment in Holliston, will cordially agree that he is very thorough and painstaking in his methods and neglects no precaution to ensure absolute accuracy in the filling of orders. Mr. Morse is a native of Holliston, and served in the army during the Rebellion, and has had over twenty five years experience in drug business. He came to Natick in 1889, and his establishment has already attained wide popularity, the methods employed in its management being highly appreciated by the purchasing public. The premises are of the dimensions of 18×65 feet, thus affording ample room for the carrying of a complete assortment of drugs, medicines and chemicals, together with a carefully chosen stock of druggists' sundries, fancy and toilet articles, cigars, confectionery, etc. Mr. Morse is a registered pharmacist and gives personal attention to the compounding of prescriptions; being prepared to fill all such orders without undue delay and at prices that are as low as is consistent with the use of pure ingredients. In fact, low rates are quoted in every department of his business, and the goods will in every instance prove precisely as represented.

Jacob Seifer, Clothes Cleaned, Repaired and Pressed, Pond Street, Natick, Mass. — This clothes cleaning establishment was founded by its present proprietor, Mr. Jacob Seifer, in 1884, and so encouraging has been his success that today he is the proprietor of the well-known works located on Pond street, and since it was thrown open to the public, has met with universal approbation and a steadily increasing business. This establishment is equipped with the latest improved facilities and every requisite for their operation. Skilled and reliable hands are employed and all work is guaranteed satisfactory. The energies of this house are devoted to the cleansing, repairing and pressing of gentlemen's garments without ripping or taking off the trimmings, and are finished to look as good as new. Clothing of all kinds is repaired in the best manner at very low prices, and all work intrusted to this establishment will be done in the most satisfactory style. Mr. Seifer is a native of Germany and is well known throughout Natick. He is an excellent business manager, whose qualifications have won for him a prominent position in this line of business, throughout the community.

Doon & Bowers, wholesale and retail dealers in Flour, Grain, Feed, Hay and Straw; Custom Grinding; Mill on Cochituate Street, Natick, Mass.—It is conceded by all in a position to judge impartially and intelligently, that Messrs. Doon & Bowers offer un-urpassed inducements to purchasers of flour, grain, feed, hay and straw, and the more thoroughly the facilities of this firm are investigated the more plainly it becomes evident that they are in a position to easily meet all honorable competition. The enterprise was inaugurated a number of years ago by Messrs. Goodnow & Wheeler, who gave place to Messrs. D. E. Wheeler & Co., the present proprietors assuming control in 1888. Mr. J. W. Doon is a native of Worcester, and Mr. C. W. Bowers of Natick, the latter gentleman having a record of nearly five years of service in the army. The firm not only deal extensively in flour, feed and similar commodities but maintain a well equipped mill on Cochituate street, where they are prepared to do custom grinding at short notice and at reasonable rates. Employment is given to three assistants, and both a wholesale and retail business is done. The firm represents the largest flour mills and grain shippers in the west, Mr. Doon being the travelling agent and prepared to fill orders by car load direct from the west to any points in the east at the very lowest wholesale rates. They carry a large stock so that the largest orders can be filled without delay. There is available, sufficient storage capacity to accommodate thirty car loads of grain, and among the commodities constantly on hand are the best brands of flour, corn, meal, ground oats, barley, shorts, fine feed, middlings, hay, straw, rye meal, wheat, cotton seed meal, mixed feed, bolted meal and Chicago gluten meal, for which Messrs. Doon & Bowers are sole agents. Their office has telephone connection and orders thus received are assured as prompt and careful attention as are those given in person.

C. A. Grattan, "Star Bakery," Catering for Parties, etc., Natick, Mass.—The plainest and most convincing proof that the people of this country are making rapid and constant gain in general culture and refinement is afforded by the class of goods in demand to-day, as compared with those which gave entire satisfaction but a few years ago. Especially noticeable is the present demand for pure and delicately flavored confectionery, and manufacturers who are able and willing to properly cater to this demand are sure of building up a prosperous business. One of the most enterprising of Natick's confectioners, is Mr. C. A. Grattan who conducts what is known as the "Star Bakery." Mr. Grattan is in a position to supply confectionery of guaranteed quality, in quantities to suit. He is a plain and fancy baker and can furnish fresh bread, cake and pastry in all its variety. The best of materials are used and the prices quoted will bear the strictest comparison with those named by other dealers in goods of equal excellence. The premises occupied are located in the Eagle Block, Main street, Natick, Mass. Employment is given to five capable and experienced assistants assuring prompt and careful attention to every order. Mr. G. S. Grattan, manager, is a native of Nova Scotia. No pains will be spared to give perfect satisfaction in all cases.

Fred L. Ward & Co., manufacturers of Men's, Boys' and Youths' Button, Lace and Congress Shoes, South Main Street, Natick, Mass.—Retail shoe dealers certainly do not need to be informed that competition is close and keen in their line of business nowadays, but some of them evidently fail to appreciate the importance of handling special goods which can be sold at moderate figures and at the same time be confidently guaranteed to prove precisely as represented. The average consumer finds more or less difficulty in getting foot-wear to suit him, and when he finally strikes an establishment where satisfactory goods are obtainable, he is bound to come again and to bring his friends, provided that the dealer makes a practice of keeping that special line in stock. Many dealers appreciate this fact, and those that do can do no better than to place their orders with Messrs. Fred L. Ward & Co., for this firm sell direct to the retail trade and make it a point to furnish goods of uniform quality. Mens', boy's and youths' button, lace and congress shoes are the specialties of this house, and their productions have always given the best of permanent satisfaction wherever introduced, both as regards their quality and their cost. Business was begun by Messrs. Lynn, Ward & Co., in 1887, the present firm being organized in 1888. It is constituted of Messrs. F. L., and C. M. Ward, both of whom are natives of Brimfield, Mass., and are thoroughly familiar with every detail of their business. The factory is conveniently located on South Main street, and sufficient assistance is employed to enable the many orders received to be promptly and accurately filled.

R. H. Randall, Dry and Fancy Goods, Ladies' Cotton Underwear a Specialty, No. 11 West Central Street, Natick, Mass.—The business indicated above was begun in 1885, and occupies premises of only about 1900 square feet, but these limited quarters are completely utilized for the accommodation of the carefully selected stock therein contained, the store is well lighted and attractively arranged and while the stock is not "immense" in quantity the proprietor has endeavored to make it select in quality, and to offer his patrons fresh and desirable goods at prices as low as is consistent with a legitimate business that intends to pay one hundred cents on a dollar. The assortment comprises a pleasing variety of dry and fancy goods with a miscellaneous stock specially designed for ladies' trade. A specialty is made of children's and ladies' underwear of which Mr. Randall is the manufacturer, and thus a producer in this community, giving employment at their homes to from twenty-five to thirty ladies, according to the season, a fact perhaps not generally known to the public, but which indicates that he is prepared to meet all honorable competition in this line for equally desirable goods. Mr. Randall is also agent for the Domestic Sewing Machine and is prepared to furnish this family favorite in various styles and prices. Mr. Randall is a native of Portland, Maine, but has conducted this enterprise here long enough to establish the fact that he is a prudent, careful and conscientious dealer who sells his goods for just what he believes them to be, and at prices that only low rent and economical running expenses would permit.

Estate of P. T. Doherty, manufacturer of Paste Stock Leather, Natick, Mass.—Of course all our readers have heard the saying so often quoted in jest and earnest—"There's nothing like leather," and yet we question if the majority of them really appreciate the wide and varied usefulness of this wonderful material. Of course its utilization in the manufacture of boots and shoes, harness, straps, trunks, bags, and such articles in common use is known to everyone, but vast as is the amount of leather consumed in these trades, there are many others which are also dependent upon this material to a greater or less extent. Very little leather is wasted nowadays, for ways have been found to utilize the smallest scraps, and it is largely owing to the ingenuity shown in this line that boots and shoes have been so reduced in cost that everybody can afford to wear them. An enormous amount of what is known as paste stock leather is annually consumed, and the demand for it is apparently bound to continue to increase for an indefinite time to come. A very large manufacturer of this material is Mr. P. T. Doherty, or rather it would be more strictly correct to say the estate of Mr. Doherty, for he carried on operations from 1879 to 1887, since which time the industry has been continued under the management of Miss Denneen, who acts as agent for the estate. The factory occupies two floors of the dimensions of 40×50 feet and the productive facilities are very large, employment being given to thirty assistants. The heaviest orders can be filled at comparatively short notice and the lowest market rates are quoted while the quality is the best.

E. M. Reed, Second-hand and Antique Furniture, No. 5 Common Street, Natick, Mass.—This enterprise is one of the novelties of the town for it might appropriately be called a "curiosity shop," for here you find the "unexpected" in various forms. Mr. Reed pays especial attention to antique furniture and anything pertaining to the household that is rare to find, whether in furniture or ornaments. His stock contains many things that have been refinished so that the original elegance has been reproduced and are now much sought for not only for their usefulness but also because they cannot be duplicated, and the fact deserves especial mention that extravagant prices are not asked for these goods, Mr. Reed being satisfied with a reasonable compensation for his time and labor. Mr. Reed deals in second-hand and antique goods, a specialty being made of the latter. The neat and attractive appearance of the stock, interspersed with the novelties on hand, impress a visitor as being quite in contrast with the general appearance of most second hand furniture stores. Mr. Reed was born in Rutland, Mass., and is a descendant of Mr. Benjamin Reed, who was one of the "minute-men in the battle of Lexington and was one of the first to surrender his life on that memorable field, and his name is now on the tablets of that field. Mr. Reed commenced business in this town under very limited circumstances, and by hard, diligent work and constant attention to business has built up a trade that is now a just reward for the effort it has cost. Mr. Reed buys second hand furniture for cash, but makes a specialty of exchange trade.

Wilson House, a Modern House, Heated by Steam, L. K. Mitchell, Proprietor, Summer Street, Natick, Mass.—The phrase "supplied with all the modern conveniences," has been so indiscriminately used that it has lost much of the meaning it originally possessed, and therefore when calling attention to the perfection of the equipment of the Wilson House, we find it necessary to state more in detail the nature of the conveniences with which it is provided. This is a modern hotel, heated by steam, supplied with electric lights, and excellently arranged from roof to basement. It is centrally and pleasantly located on Summer street, and contains thirty five sleeping rooms which are comfortably furnished and are constantly kept in the very best of condition. The proprietor, Mr. L. K. Mitchell, has had charge of the house for about five years and has built up an enviable reputation for liberality and honorable dealing, as he spares no pains to make his guests feel entirely at home and is uniformly moderate in his charges. Employment is afforded to six efficient assistants, and due courtesy to every patron is insisted upon under all circumstances. The table is bountifully provided for, being supplied with an extensive variety of seasonable food at all times of year, and the bill of fare is made up with such care that it seems as if all tastes must surely be satisfied, especially as the cooking is equal to the best. Such of our readers as have occasion to visit Natick for a long or short period and have no regular hotel, should make it a point to try the accommodations offered at the Wilson House, and we are confident that those who do will thank us for calling their attention to so comfortable a stopping place.

—

Charles H. Whitcomb, Our Hatter, Gents' Furnishings, Trunks, Valises, Lap Robes, Horse Clothing, etc. Nobscot Block, South Framingham. 13 Clark's Block, Natick, Mass.—Such of our readers as wish to see an extensive and skillfully chosen assortment of hats, caps, gentlemen's furnishings, etc., would do well to call at one of the establishments conducted by Mr. Charles H. Whitcomb, for he carries on two stores—one in this town and the other in Nobscot Block, South Framingham, Mass., and at either of these places there is to be found a stock which will repay careful inspection. Mr. Whitcomb certainly does not lack experience, for he has been identified with his present line of business ever since 1867, and one result of this experience is his ability to meet all honorable competition by furnishing desirable goods at positively bottom prices. The Natick store is located at No. 13 Clark's Block, and is occupied in conjunction with Mr. A. W. Palmer, a prominent dealer in clothing, so that one may order an entire outfit of wearing apparel without leaving the premises. Mr. Whitcomb caters to no special class of trade, but carries a stock suited to all tastes and to all purses. Besides hats and gents' furnishings it includes trunks, valises, lap robes, horse clothing, etc., and is kept constantly complete in every department. Employment is given to three efficient assistants and callers are assured immediate and painstaking attention, uniformly polite service being the rule to all.

W. E. Daniels Hack, Boarding, Sale and Livery Stable. Barges Furnished for Picnics and Excursions. Also Hacks for Weddings and Funerals. Landau, with experienced driver, for Private parties; 45 Summer Street, Natick, Mass. —Few things are more provoking than to order hacks for any public occasion, such as a wedding, a party, or a funeral, and have some ramshackle, worn-out vehicle sent along in which anyone who has a decent regard for appearances is ashamed to ride. The average person does not have very frequent occasion to place such orders and hence is not apt to be well posted as to where they may be placed to the best advantage, so that such of our readers as are included in this category and wish to ensure against being furnished with any such vehicles as we have referred to, would do well to bear in mind that Mr. W. E. Daniels of No. 45 Summer street, gives particular attention to the furnishing of hacks for weddings and funerals, and is prepared to supply vehicles that will prove satisfactory to the most fastidious, notwithstanding that his charges are moderate in every instance. Mr. Daniels also furnishes barges for picnics and excursions, and maintains a landau with an experienced and careful driver, for the use of private parties. He also carries on a general jobbing and furniture moving business. He is a native of Vermont, and succeeded Mr. C. H. Shermen in the ownership of his present establishment in 1881. In addition to the services already mentioned Mr. Daniels provides desirable teams for livery purposes; filling orders without delay and at low rates. He takes horses to board, guaranteeing them comfortable quarters and suitable care; and as he carries on quite an extensive sale business, those wishing to purchase a reliable animal at a fair price would do well to give him a call.

J. B. Fairbanks & Son, dealers in Fancy Goods, Toys and Notions, Books, Stationery, etc., 16 Main Street, Natick, Mass.—In pursuing our investigations to obtain material to compound this volume, the facts are prominently brought before us that thousands of operatives and hundreds of thousands of capital are invested in the manufacture of fancy goods, toys, etc., and, furthermore, that the lines of goods offered for sale in the Natick stores are fully equal, and in many cases, superior in quality and finish to those displayed elsewhere. Of the houses concerned in this vast industry, we will now devote a space to the one presided over by Mr. J. B. Fairbanks & Son. This establishment was opened in 1865 by Mr. J. B. Fairbanks, Mr. George C. Fairbanks having been admitted as partner to the business about 1870. The premises occupied are located at No. 16 Main street, and are 25×70 feet in dimensions. The stock dealt in comprises fancy goods, toys and notions of all kinds. In addition to the above named goods, Messrs. Fairbanks & Son deal in books, stationery, etc., and conduct an extensive retail trade in their lines of goods. Mr. J. B. Fairbanks is a native of Medfield, Mass., and Mr. George C. Fairbanks of Natick. Both these gentlemen are well known in social as well as business circles. Mr. J. B. Fairbanks was connected with the school committee and was representative for two years, and Mr. George C. Fairbanks has held the office of auditor for two years.

John Carrigan, Dining Rooms and Home Cooking. South Avenue, opposite Depot, Natick, Mass.—These popular dining rooms are accessible, quiet, neat, well lighted, airy and comfortable; the food is the best that the market affords, the cooking is first class and the service prompt and obliging. Many of our readers do not need to be informed that the above is an accurate description of Mr. John Carrigan's dining rooms, and this being so, the fact that they are the most popular in Natick follows as a necessary consequence. Mr. Carrigan has always shown great enterprise in catering to the wants of his patrons since he assumed entire control in 1889, and has greatly enlarged the business. The premises utilized are located on South avenue, opposite the depot, and afford a very desirable place for ladies and their escorts to lunch, dine or partake of some of the many delicacies to be obtained here, and for which this establishment is noted. It is located opposite the depot and is very largely patronized by suburban "shoppers" as well as by residents of this place. Forty guests can be seated at a time, and are constantly served by the six competent assistants who are constantly in attendance. Strangers visiting Natick would do well to remember that the best place to get a regular meal or a lunch is at the dining rooms conducted by Mr. John Carrigan and located directly opposite the depot, for the "home cooking" is first-class and the charges very moderate, considering the quality of the food supplied and the service rendered.

Thomas L. Irwin, "The Natick House Furnisher," Eagle Block, Main Street, Natick, Mass.—There is no need of argument to establish the fact that an enterprise which has a tendency to encourage people to go to housekeeping and thus establish homes of their own is a good thing for the community at large, and as the undertaking carried on by Mr. Thomas L. Irwin exercises a powerful influence in this direction it is deserving of especially prominent and favorable mention as a genuine public benefit. The proprietor is a native of Northampton, Mass., and succeeded Mr. C. H. Robinson in the ownership of the enterprise in question in 1877. Mr. Irwin is familiarly and very generally known as "the Natick House Furnisher," and the title is thoroughly well-deserved, for he is prepared to furnish any kind of a house from cellar to attic and to do the job as promptly, as cheaply and in every way as satisfactorily as any one in the business. We do not ask our readers to take our word for this, but simply request them to look into the matter for themselves. Call at Mr. Irwin's store in Eagle Block, examine the heavy and varied stock, note the prices, see how the goods compare in quality with those offered elsewhere, and then draw your own conclusions. Four floors, having an area of some 5,000 square feet are utilized, and the assortment on hand is always seasonable and attractive. Sufficient assistance is employed to ensure prompt and careful attention to every caller, and we may add that no one is importuned to buy, goods being gladly shown at all times. Mr. Irwin is prepared to sell both for cash and on installments so there is no reason why all should not take advantage of the inducements he offers. His establishment is a thoroughly representative one and is a prime, popular favorite throughout this vicinity.

Mrs. John Kenealy, Dry and Fancy Goods, Gents' Furnishing Goods, Men's, Youths' and Boys' Underwear, South Main Street, Down's New Block, Natick, Mass.—The ladies of Natick have certainly no good reason to complain of the "shopping" facilities afforded them, for there are a number of enterprising houses engaged in the dry and fancy goods business in this town, and the attractions offered and the prices quoted by some of these firms will compare favorably with those attainable in Boston or any other large trade centre. Among the most reliable of the houses in question stands that conducted now by Mrs. John Kenealy, and a discriminating purchaser only needs to visit this ladies' store on South Main street (Down's New Block) to become convinced that the values there offered are genuine and even exceptional. The business was founded by Mr. John Kenealy, and since 1889, has been under the able management of Mrs Kenealy. The premises utilized are about 800 feet in dimensions and an extensive retail business is done, requiring the services of two competent assistants. The stock comprises dry and fancy goods, collars, cuffs, gents' furnishing goods, also men's, youths' and boys' underwear, including the very latest novelties in these several lines as well as a full selection of staple products. The service is prompt, reliable and obliging, the prices are as low as the lowest, and the goods are in every instance warranted to prove just as represented. Mrs. Kenealy also is a practical dress maker and gives painstaking attention to all branches of this business, she also carries a good line of ladies' wrappers.

Washington Street Stables, Edmond Ryan, Proprietor. Horses Boarded, Baited, Sold or Exchanged. First-class Hacks for Weddings and Funerals. Barges Furnished for Parties and Excursions. Carriages for Sale, Natick, Mass.—The enterprise conducted by Mr. Edmond Ryan was carried on for more than fifteen years by Mr. M. W. Hayward before the present proprietor assumed control in 1887, and has long ranked among the leading undertakings of the kind in the State. The Washington Street Stables contain forty stalls, are illuminated by electricity, and are equipped throughout in first-class style; employment being given to seven assistants and all orders being assured immediate and painstaking attention. Horses taken to board are assured comfortable quarters, an abundance of good food and the best of care, the charges made in this department of the business being uniformly moderate. First-class hacks will be furnished for weddings, funerals and other public occasions; and barges for parties and excursions with careful and expert drivers will also be supplied at short notice and at low rates. Mr. Ryan is native of Stowe, Mass., and has a very large circle of friends in this vicinity. He gives close personal attention to the supervision of affairs and is constantly striving to improve the service rendered. A large sale and exchange business in horses is carried on, and carriages are also dealt in, thoroughly dependable vehicles being offered at positively bottom prices. Orders for wheelwright work and carriage painting will be filled in a thoroughly satisfactory manner at short notice, and as the premises have have telephone connection communications can be quickly and easily sent from any point in this vicinity.

H. Harwood & Sons manufacturers of Base Balls, Natick, Mass.—We are accustomed to speak of base ball as the "National game," and the vast amount of space given it during the playing season by the leading newspapers of the country indicates the great popularity it enjoys among all classes of people, but in order to get some kind of an adequate idea of the extent to which the game is indulged in, it is necessary to visit such an establishment as that conducted by Messrs. H. Harwood & Sons in this town. This concern are among the most extensive and best-known base ball manufacturers in the country and their business is of exceptionally long standing for one of its character, having been founded in 1858, or long before the game had attained any great prominence. The factory occupies three floors of the dimensions of 35×90 feet and is equipped with all necessary facilities for the manufacture of base balls of all kinds, for there is as much difference in base balls as there is in shoes, the retail price varying from five cents to $1.25. Messrs. H. Harwood & Sons turn out a very complete line and their goods are handled by the leading dealers throughout the country. Employment is given to from 150 to 200 assistants, and several thousand barrels of balls are made every year, the demand being steadily on the increase. The productions of this factory will compare favorably with those of any other of a like nature in the Union, both as regards variety and the uniform excellence of each grade. The firm are prepared to fill orders promptly and to quote the lowest market rates at all times.

C. M. McKechnie, dealer in Domestic and Vienna Bread, Cake and Pastry. Ice Cream a Specialty. No. 10 Main Street, opposite the bank, Natick, Mass.—Housework is none too easy, even under the most favorable circumstances, and every housekeeper knows that the baking of bread, cake and pastry is one of the most troublesome and difficult of all her duties. Since the establishment of this bakery which Mr. C. M. McKechnie has conducted for more than five years, many have abandoned baking their own bread, etc., and there is no question but that many more would do the same thing if they were aware of the uniform excellence of Mr. McKechnie's products, and realized that they would not only save time, but money also, by so doing. There were some who had a prejudice against "baker's bread" when this establishment began operations, but they found that the goods offered were just as clean, just as carefully made, and, in short, just as good as the *best* home-made articles, and far superior to the average. The premises occupied are located at No. 10 Main street, Natick, opposite the bank. It comprises one floor measuring 18×70 feet, with a bakery in the rear. The proprietor is familiar with every detail of his business, and gives it his close personal supervision, uses the best materials and spares no pains to produce goods that will suit the most fastidious. Employment is given to five capable assistants. He has constantly on hand domestic and Vienna bread, cake and pastry. He makes a specialty of ice cream and of catering for weddings, parties, etc. Prompt and of careful attention is given to all orders.

J. O. Wilson & Co. manufacturers of Mens', Boys' and Youth's Brogans and Plow Shoes, Natick, Mass.—The manufacture of boots and shoes is so extensively carried on in Natick and vicinity that an establishment devoted to their production must have marked distinctive features in order to entitle it to special mention, and a prominent example of such an establishment is that conducted by Messrs. J. O. Wilson & Co., this factory being one of the largest and best-appointed of the kind in this section of the State. The premises utilized include one portion comprising three stories and a basement, another two stories and a basement, and a spacious ell, the entire factory being fitted up with improved machinery and employment being given to from 400 to 500 operatives. Every detail of this vast business is given careful and skillful supervision and the consequence is there is less trouble and confusion than is often met with in the management of much less extensive undertakings. The capacity of the factory is about 6,000 pairs per day, and the product is in such active demand that the firm find this not a bit too large, particularly during the busy season. Messrs. J. O. Wilson & Co. manufacture men's, boys' and youths' brogans and plow shoes and their goods have an unsurpassed reputation for strength and durability, being prime favorites with consumers wherever introduced. This business was founded more than a quarter of a century ago, and has gained its present magnitude by a steady process of development. It was at one time conducted by Messrs. J. O. Wilson & Son, but the existing proprietors are Messrs. J. O. Wilson and H. G. Wood, both of whom are natives of New Hampshire and are widely known in trade circles.

P. F. Doherty, Groceries, Flour and Grain, South Main Street, Natick, Mass.—Among the retail dealers in groceries, flour and grain doing business in this section, no one occupies a more prominent position than does Mr. P. F. Doherty, and the extent of his operations is significantly indicated by the magnitude of his stock, it being one of the largest in town. The establishment in question is located on South Main street and is 20×60 feet in dimensions, and was originally established by Mr. Thomas Donnellon, who was succeeded by T. M. Lynch, the present proprietor having assumed entire control in 1889. Mr. Doherty is a native of Natick, and very well known throughout this vicinity. The advantages gained by dealing with a house carrying a heavy and varied stock at all times, are obvious enough to require no explanation, and the steadily growing popularity of the establishment in question shows that the public appreciate the inducements there offered. Enjoying highly favorable relations with producers, Mr. Doherty is in a position to quote low prices as well as to supply dependable goods, and in the sale of certain indispensable commodities, such as groceries, flour, grain, etc., he takes especial pains to satisfy the most critical customers, both as regards the quality of the product and the prices named on the same. All orders are promptly filled, and large or small buyers are assured equal consideration.

The Union Beef Co.'s Famous Market E. M. Wall, Manager, Downs' Block, Natick, Mass.—The Union Beef Company have their headquarters at Holliston, but since they opened their Natick branch, in 1889, their business has developed with surprising rapidity, for the residents of this town are quick to appreciate solid advantages, and the liberal support they give the new enterprise cannot but be gratifying to Messrs. Coughlin Brothers the proprietors, and Mr. E. M. Wall, the manager. The company do both a wholesale and retail business, and carry a very heavy stock at both their stores; that in this town being located in Downs' Block, and having an area of 1,000 square feet. The company evidently find that it pays to keep good faith with their customers, for they never make an announcement not justified by the facts, and they spare no pains to completely satisfy every patron. No matter what you require in the line of meats and provisions the chances are that they can supply it, and what is still more to the point, that they can and will quote lower prices than any other dealers in this vicinity. Sufficient assistance is employed to fill orders without that exasperating delay so common in this line of business, and equal courtesy is extended to every buyer, large or small.

J. B. Sweeny, Harness-Maker, Summer Street, Natick.—There is no recreation more safe than that of driving provided it be carried on under proper conditions, but considering the careless ness displayed by many who indulge in the sport the wonder is that accidents are not doubly as frequent as they now are. No competent judge can examine some of the harnesses offered for sale as "great bargains" without feeling that certain manufacturers care more for money than for life, for inferior stock and poor workman ship are not at all liable to stand sudden strains or hard usage, and a broken trace, hold back strap, or rein is one of the most fruitful causes of serious accident. One reason why we take pleasure in calling attention to the harness and horse furnishings offered by Mr. J. B. Sweeny, doing business on Summer street, is because we are confident that he sells things precisely on their merits, never misrepresenting them under any circumstances. Then again his prices are uniformly moderate, and his stock is large and varied enough to enable all orders to be promptly filled. Mr. Sweeny is a practical harness-maker and is prepared to do custom-work and repairing in a neat and durable manner at short notice. His charges are reasonable in every instance, and carefully selected material is used, no pains being spared to fully maintain the enviable rep utation attained in connection with this impor tant department of the business.

Miss C. A. Travis, Millinery and Worsteds, 19 Main Street, Clark's Block, Natick, Mass.— This establishment has long been known as hold ing a leading position among similar enterprises in this section. This house was first introduced to the public in 1867, under the name of Travis & Washburn and so continued until 1870, when Miss Travis became the sole proprietress and has conducted the business in a highly satisfactory manner both for herself and her numerous pat rons. Miss Travis occupies part of the store located at 19 Main street, Clark's Block, with G. L. Bartlett, dry goods. She has in her employ five competent assistants during the season, and is well prepared to fill all orders at reasonable notice. It is hardly necessary to speak in detail concerning the advantages gained by placing millinery orders here, as it is very generally un derstood by the ladies of Natick and vicinity that Miss Travis' taste is unsurpassed, and that she is very successful in suiting her work to the individuality of the purchaser. She keeps thoroughly well informed concerning the latest dictates of fashion, and her stock is replete with novelties in every department. She has also a fine assortment of worsteds which she is happy to show to those wishing for such goods. Her charges are moderate and satisfaction may be confidently expected by every customer.

F. R. Leland, House Painting, Graining and Paper Hanging, opposite the Common, Natick, Mass.—It is true economy to keep frame build ings well painted, and those who think to save money by pursuing a contrary course, are sure to be disappointed, for the matter is now too thoroughly understood to admit of any uncer tainty whatever. New England weather is about as destructive as anything of the kind can be, and the protection afforded to wood work by a couple of good coats of paint is enough to jus tify the expense of it, leaving the question of appearances entirely aside. It requires good stock and skillful application to ensure the best results, and both of these may be provided for by placing orders with Mr. F. R. Leland, for this gentleman makes a speciality of house paint ing, graining and paper hanging, and does work equal to the best, at uniformly reasonable rates. A sufficient number of assistants are employed to enable immediate and satisfactory attention to be given to every order, and there is no reasona ble room to doubt that the high reputation gained in the past, will be maintained in the future. Large or small orders are given equal considera tion and estimates will be cheerfully and care fully made on application.

James Downs, Baker and Caterer, Downs' Block, Natick, Mass.—There are few residents in Natick who are not more or less familiar with the establishment of Mr. James Downs, which for many years has been prominently before the public as headquarters for anything in the line of the baker and caterer. This house was founded by S. B. Blethin in 1872, who was succeeded in 1877 by the present proprietor. The premises occupied for the transaction of this business are located in Downs' Block and are 20×60 feet in dimensions. The energies of this house are de voted to the wholesale and retail trade in all kinds of baker's products, of which only the finest grades are manufactured. Mr. Downs gives special attention to the catering business in all its branches, and orders for parties, weddings, etc., will be executed in the most prompt and satisfactory manner. Employment is given to four thoroughly skilled and experienced assist ants, and all orders are promptly filled and accu rately delivered to any part of Natick. In all departments of this business there is noticeably a marked orderly and systematic method for the proper and correct conduct of each operation of the work, thereby ensuring first class results.

Brooks & Gleason, Boarding and Livery Stable. Horses and Carriages to Let. Hacks Furnished with careful and experienced drivers. Particular attention given to Boarding Horses and Furnishing Carriages for parties. No. 28 Summer Street, Natick, Mass.—A thoroughly well-appointed and well-managed stable is one of the most useful establishments that can be carried on in any community, and the residents of Natick and vicinity have excellent reason to congratulate themselves that the town is so well provided for in this respect as is the case at present, for the stable conducted by Messrs. Brooks & Gleason at No. 28 Summer street, is one of the best to be found in this section of the State, and the management spare no pains to keep the service rendered at the very highest standard of efficiency. This enterprise had its inception many years ago, and has changed hands repeatedly, the original proprietor being Mr. C. H. Sherman, who was succeeded by Messrs. Clark & Brooks, they giving place to Mr. R. T. Brooks, who retained sole control for more than a score of years, finally being succeeded by Mr. C. T. Brooks in June, 1888, and the present firm was formed in December, 1889; the partners being Messrs. C. T. Brooks and L. E. Gleason. The former is a native of Natick, Mass., and the latter of Wayland, Mass., Mr. Gleason being well known hereabouts, as he was formerly the proprietor of the Wilson House in this town. Both members of the firm give close personal attention to the supervision of affairs and propose to develop the business in every department if offering a superior service at moderate rates will do it. A specialty is made of boarding horses and furnishing carriages for parties, and as there are some fifty stalls on the premises extensive facilities are available. Hacks will be furnished, with competent and careful drivers, at short notice, and an extensive livery trade is carried on, some stylish, easy-riding and in every way desirable turnouts being provided for use in this department, while the charges made are uniformly reasonable.

L. P. Stone, dealer in all Kinds of Provisions, Masonic Block, Natick, Mass.—This is a very popular establishment for its proprietor, Mr. L. P. Stone, knows what the public want, and has a way of so satisfactorily supplying that want, that those who trade with him once, are pretty sure to come again, and, after a while, to induce their friends to come also. Mr. Stone is a native of Natick, Mass., and founded his present business in 1885. He is so well known throughout this vicinity that extended personal mention is quite unnecessary. This house occupies one floor 25×70 feet in dimensions, and a basement, and at all times contains a very full assortment of meats, vegetables, canned goods, dairy products, eggs, etc., these goods being carefully selected for family trade, and being quoted at prices which will bear the severest comparison with those named at any retail provision store in this neighborhood, for Mr. Stone believes in selling at low figures, preferring the "nimble penny" to the "slow sixpence." There are two competent and obliging assistants employed, and callers may be sure of receiving prompt and polite attention, for large and small buyers are shown equal consideration, and no trouble is spared to satisfy everybody.

Daniels & Twitchell, Prescription Pharmacists, Natick, Mass.—The business conducted by the firm of Daniels & Twitchell has held its present prominent position for so long a time, that it is safe to say no one at all familiar with Natick's business houses can be unacquainted with it, and indeed we question if there is a concern in the town engaged in a similar line of trade which is more generally and favorably known. This business was started about twenty-one years ago by Mr. S. O. Daniels, and in 1888 Mr. F. B. Twitchell became connected with the business as manager. There is probably no other branch of trade known to commerce in which so great a responsibility is incurred as there is in that carried on by the druggist. Dealing as he does, in drugs and chemicals, unfamiliar to the general public, many of which agents are deadly in their effects when used in certain quantities, or when combined improperly with other materials, he must rely absolutely and entirely on the knowledge, care and skill of himself and employes for the assurance that by no fault of his, or those for whom he is morally, if not legally responsible, shall the life, or even the comfort, of the hundreds whom he daily serves, be endangered. We need go no farther than the establishment of Daniels & Twitchell, located at No. 25 Main street, for an example of what a prescription pharmacist should be. The dimensions of this store are 24×70 feet and it contains a valuable stock of drugs and chemicals of all kinds. Employment is given to three competent assistants. Prescriptions may be left with this firm with the moral certainty that all that learning, skill and improved apparatus can do toward obtaining satisfactory results, will be done by those to whom they are entrusted.

A. I. & G. W. Travis & Co., manufacturers of Men's, Boys' and Youths' Kip, Split and Grain Boots, Brogans, Bals. and Plow Shoes, Natick, Mass.—One of the oldest established enterprises of the kind in this town is that carried on by Messrs. A. I. & G. W. Travis & Co., for this was inaugurated nearly forty years ago, operations being begun by Messrs. C. B. Travis & Co., in 1852. This firm was succeeded by Messrs. Damon, Thomas & Lewis, they by Mr. C. W. Copeland, he by Mr. R. W. Cone, who gave place to the existing concern in 1886. The present proprietors are Messrs. A. I. and G. W. Travis, both of whom are natives of this town. The factory is a commodious and well-arranged structure, containing three floors and measuring 60 × 80 feet. Employment is afforded to fifty assistants, and the product averages some 600 pairs per day, being composed entirely of heavy goods especially designed for the southern and western trade. The firm manufacture men's, boys' and youths' kip, split and grain boots, brogans, balmorals and plow shoes, and are in a position to fill orders promptly and to quote bottom prices at all times. Their productions are very widely known among the trade, and the constant demand for them is the best possible evidence of their standard merit. A full line of samples is carried at No. 120 Summer street, Boston, but all correspondence should be addressed to Natick.

Robinson & Jones, dealers in Coal and Wood, Bundle Hay and Straw. Wood Sawed and Prepared to Order. Office and Yard, Union Court, Natick, Mass.—One of the oldest established and most truly representative enterprises of the kind in Natick and vicinity is that carried on by Messrs. Robinson & Jones, dealers in coal and wood, bundle hay and straw. This was inaugurated many years ago by Mr. John S. Wood, who was succeeded in 1857 by Mr. Henry Goodnow, he giving place to the existing firm in 1867. The proprietors are Messrs. C. H. Jones and W. B. Robinson, and are among the best-known of our local business men. The firm do a very extensive retail business; their main office and yard being located in Union Court, Natick, and branch establishments being maintained at Cochituate and at Saxonville. The Natick premises can accommodate about 3,000 tons of coal, those in Cochituate about 1,000 tons, and those in Saxonville a smaller amount. Employment is given to twelve assistants, and any of the commodities dealt in will be delivered at any point in this vicinity at short notice, and at prices strictly in accordance with the lowest market rates. Wood will be sawed and cut to any dimensions desired, and equally careful attention is assured to large and small orders, the firm having an enviable reputation for extending uniform courtesy to every customer. Coal will be weighed on the town scales if it is requested. It is the endeavor of the firm that all orders be delivered promptly, all errors gladly corrected, and satisfaction guaranteed.

Chas. W. Ambrose, Watchmaker and Jeweler. Watches, Jewelry, French and American Clocks, Skillfully and Promptly Repaired, 15 Clark's Block, Natick, Mass.—The general introduction of machine made watches, and perfection of a system which so operates as to keep each workman in a watch factory doing the same thing over and over again, have of course resulted in the cost of reliable time keepers being very materially lessened, and so are worthy of unstinted approval, but they have other effects which are not so gratifying, and one of the most annoying of these is the present scarcity of really skillful practical watch makers, and the consequent difficulty experienced in having fine watches repaired properly. There are probably none of our readers who have carried a fine chronometer for any length of time but what have met with the difficulty mentioned, and they at all events will be pleased to learn of an establishment where fine watch repairing is made a specialty and where the very best work is done at moderate rates. We refer to that conducted by Mr. Chas. W. Ambrose, at No. 15 Clark's Block, Natick. Without asserting for a moment that this is the only place where first-class repairing is done, it may still be said that no better work of the kind is done in this vicinity, and few establishments enjoy so high a position in connection with the filling of such orders. Mr. Ambrose occupies the store in connection with Mr. James H. Frost, who is a druggist. Mr. Ambrose gives his personal attention to his business, which consists of jewelry as well as watches, also French and American clocks, which can be skillfully and promptly repaired.

J. F. Gray, Confectioner and Caterer, Masonic Block, Natick, Mass.—No one can compare the candies in the market to-day with those offered a decade or so ago, without being struck with the great advance which has been made in this line of manufacture, for it is unquestionably true that the confectionery of to-day is, generally speaking, decidedly purer, more carefully manufactured, and more delicately flavored than any which has preceded it. The public demand pure and skillfully made confectionery, and those manufacturers who have the ability to appreciate this demand, and the enterprise to cater to it, are of course the ones who do the most extensive business. In this connection we may very appropriately call attention to the establishment carried on by Mr. J. F. Gray, who is located in Masonic Block, for this gentleman is a manufacturer of pure confections, and he spares no pains to suit the most fastidious customers, and who carries on an extensive retail business. Mr. Gray commenced business in New Bedford, Mass., in 1862, and removed to Natick where he has since remained, in 1884. The premises occupied measure 15×70 feet, where he has every facility for attending to orders of his customers, as caterer, or to fill orders for ice cream or fruit. He has three able assistants and all orders will be filled with care and promptness, and at the lowest rates for pure unadulterated articles.

H. F. Chamberlin, Dry and Fancy Goods. No. 6 Main Street, Natick, Mass.—The business carried on by Mr. H. F. Chamberlin at No. 6 Main street, was founded about half a century ago, this enterprise being the oldest one of the kind in Natick. The present proprietor only assumed control in 1889, but he has been very prominently identified with the undertaking for a score of years, during which time he officiated as head clerk for the former owners, Messrs. P. F. Woodbury & Co. Mr. Chamberlin is a native of this town and is one of the best known of all our local business men, both in social and in trade circles. Considering his long and varied experience, it goes without saying that he is thoroughly familiar with every detail of the business, and as he give it close personal attention the service is maintained at the very highest standard of efficiency. The premises utilized are 25×75 feet in dimensions, exclusive of a spacious cloak room, and contain a heavy and carefully chosen assortment of imported and domestic dry and fancy goods, comprising the very latest fashionable novelties, and being remarkably complete in every department. The most discriminating buyers residing in Natick and vicinity, make it a rule to visit this popular store when anything in the line of dry or fancy goods is wanted, and we need hardly say that the enviable reputation for enterprise and honorable dealing so long associated with this representative undertaking is fully maintained under the present management. Dependable goods, bottom prices, prompt and polite service to all—this makes a strong combination and fully explains the popularity of this deserving enterprise. Notwithstanding the magnitude of the business there is no delay in serving customers, for efficient assistants are employed and immediate and courteous attention is the rule to all.

Miss A. F. McGrath, Millinery and Fancy Goods, cor. Main and Pond Streets, Natick, Mass. —We believe that Natick, Mass., is not surpassed by any place of its population in New England as regards the number and excellence of the millinery establishments it contains, and yet the business is far from being overcrowded—that is to say as far as strictly first class milliners are concerned. It may be freely admitted that a milliner of ordinary skill and enterprise has not so much chance of success here as in a score of places that might be named, but that this is true only of those having no special qualifications is shown by the success which has attended Miss A. F. McGrath since she began operations in 1885. This lady has already built up an extensive and highly desirable patronage, and every indication seems to point to continued success. The premises occupied are located at the corner of Main and Pond streets, Natick, and have an area of about 600 feet. It is well arranged and contains a fine assortment of millinery and fancy goods in general, both of foreign and domestic origin. Miss McGrath employes two experienced assistants and gives personal attention to the filling of orders for custom work. Satisfaction is warranted to all customers. Trimmed and untrimmed hats and bonnets, ribbons, velvets, feathers, ornaments, flowers, etc., are offered in great variety.

Newell Cooper, Shirt Manufacturer, Washington Street, Natick, Mass.—The phenomenal popularity which fancy woolen shirts have attained of late years speaks well for the sound common sense of the public, for these shirts are admirable from a hygienic point of view and combine beauty, utility and comfortableness to an exceptional degree. It is to be deplored that some so called "cheap" shirts of this kind have lately been placed upon the market, for these are really cheap only in name and are so badly made from inferior material that they cannot give satisfaction and are liable to prejudice many against outing and tourist's shirts of all kinds. An excellent example of a precisely opposite policy is that afforded by the methods employed by Mr. Newell Cooper, who is extensively engaged in shirt manufacturing in this town. Mr. Cooper was born in Maine, and served in the army during the Rebellion. He has carried on his present enterprise for about ten years and his productions now have a standard reputation which assures for them a ready sale. An entire building of the dimensions of 24×40 feet is utilized, it being equipped with all necessary machinery run by steam power. Employment is given to from thirty to forty assistants, and Mr. Cooper manufactures for Boston parties and makes a specialty of woolen and outing shirts and shows many new and attractive patterns.

HOWE CEMENT COMPANY, NORWICH, CONN.

The Howe Cement Co., manufacturers of Fine Shoe Dressings, 32 Talman Street, Norwich, Conn.—It will never be known exactly how many thousands of dollars have been spent in the improvement of cements for leather, rubber, etc., but the total sum must be very large indeed for almost numberless attempts have been made to discover new compounds, and experiments have been carried on for prolonged periods and almost without regard to expense. The ideal cement is unaffected by moisture or a reasonable degree of heat, hardens quickly, but not too quickly, is easily applied and contains no ingredient in the least degree harmful to leather or rubber. In the opinion of many practical men and thoroughly competent judges, the compounds produced by the Howe Cement Company more nearly approach this ideal than any others in the market, and the proof of this is to be found in the large and rapidly increasing demand for the company's goods. Operations

were begun in 1874, and the business has increased until now three floors of dimensions averaging 30×25 feet each are utilized for manufacturing purposes, and employment is given to a number of experienced assistants. The office and factory are located at No. 32 Talman street, and are equipped with all necessary facilities for the manufacture of leather and rubber cements, thus enabling orders to be filled at short notice and at moderate rates. The company also manufacture the celebrated DAISY SHOE POLISH which is warranted perfectly harmless to ladies' and children's fine shoes and gives a durable and brilliant gloss. It is put up in attractive form, and if desired it can be procured in a wooden safety box which prevents breakage. They also manufacture the EAGLE DRESSING, which is equally harmless and the best ten cent dressing made. The proprietors are Messrs. S, G, and W. K. Howe, the former being a native of Maine and the latter of Massachusetts.

HISTORICAL SKETCH

OF

COCHITUATE, MASS.

The flourishing village of Cochituate is located on the southern border of the town of Wayland and is now just about sixty years old, its origin dating back to 1830, when Messrs. William and J. M. Bent began the manufacture of shoes.

Although comparatively young when considered in connection with other Massachusetts villages, it is yet older than the town in which it is located, for Wayland has borne its present name only since 1835. But when the date of the grant and settlement of this territory is taken into consideration it is found that it is one of the oldest of Massachusett's plantations, it embracing about two-thirds of the tract granted in 1637 by the General Court as the township of Sudbury. The present Sudbury lies entirely on the west side of the Sudbury River, and is made up of one-third of the original grant of land and subsequent additions. The original village of Sudbury was on the east side of the river, and for about ninety years the town meeting-house, corn-mill, grave-yard, and in fact all the public and semi-public Sudbury institutions were located on that side, but in 1780 the town was divided, that part on the west bank taking the name of Sudbury, and that on the east bank being henceforth known as East Sudbury, until the name Wayland was adopted about fifty-five years ago.

The existing township has an area of 10,051 acres and is bounded on the north by Lincoln, on the east by Weston and on the south by Natick, the Sudbury River forming its western boundary for a distance of five miles and 251 rods, and having a total length, within the town limits, of 10 miles and 162 rods.

As a town, Wayland is to be classed among distinctively agricultural communities, and the Sudbury River meadows have been profitably cultivated from the very beginning. The town was named in honor of Francis Wayland, D.D., president of Brown University, who to show his appreciation of the compliment offered to give $500, provided the town furnished an equal amount, and used the combined sum in the founding of a library which should be for the free use of all the inhabitants. The gift was accepted, but as the question was raised whether the town had a legal right to raise money by tax for such a purpose, a larger sum than had been appropriated was raised by private subscription and given to the town to be used in establishing a library. In this connection it is interesting to note that the general law under which free libraries have been founded throughout the State was passed through the influence of Wayland's representative in 1851, Rev. John B. Wight.

The town library was founded in 1848 and opened for the delivery of books in 1850, it being the first free public library in Massachusetts.

STREET IN COCHITUATE, MASS.

As before stated, the village of Cochituate owes its origin and much of its development to Messrs. William, and J. M. Bent, who were the pioneer shoe manufacturers. The village takes its name from its location on Lake Cochituate,—the main source of Boston's water supply.

The growth of shoe manufacturing within its borders during a period of less than forty years is shown by the following figures :

The number of pairs of shoes manufactured in 1837 was 29,660, value, $22,419 ; males employed, thirty-one ; females, fifteen. In 1875 the value of manufactured goods was $1,799,175 ; males employed, 431 ; females sixty. The statistics for the last fifteen years show a generally steady and pronounced gain, and indicate that the prosperity of the village is not so easily influenced by disturbing causes as is that of most manufacturing communities. Of course any national "boom" or depression is bound to influence local industries to some extent, but the balance is not so sensitive here as at many other points, and the equipment and general facilities of the more prominent local manufacturers are of a character that enables them to meet all honorable competition in the markets where their productions are best known and most largely in demand. The future of the village looks as bright as its past has been prosperous, and a continuance of the energy which has thus far characterized the management of its industries will doubtless assure steady and solid development.

LEADING BUSINESS MEN

OF

COCHITUATE.

Wm. & J. M. Bent, manufacturers of Fine Shoes, Cochituate, Mass.—There are evidences on every hand of the wonderful progress which has been made of late years in shoe manufacturing, but in order to really appreciate the perfection which has been attained in this line of industry it is necessary to visit such an establishment as is conducted by Messrs. Wm. & J. M. Bent here in Cochituate, for this is one of the largest and best-equipped factories devoted to the production of fine shoes in the entire country, and the product is accepted as the standard of quality in all markets in which it has been introduced. This great business has been built up from very modest beginnings and has been fully sixty years in attaining its present magnitude, operations having been begun in 1830, by Mr. William Bent, and the existing firm-name having been adopted in 1849. The present proprietors assumed control in 1885, and consist of Messrs. William H., J. A., Myron W. and Ralph Bent, and are sons of Mr. J. M. Bent, and became identified with the business at the date last given. All are natives of this town, and Wm. H. and J. A. have served on the board of selectmen, and Wm. H. and M. W. have served as representatives. They give careful personal attention to the management of the vast undertaking with which their names are identified, and as a consequence the elaborate plant of machinery is maintained at the very highest standard of efficiency, and the work turned out has no superior in the world in its special line. The main shop is four stories in height and 100×45 feet in dimensions, see cut on page 84, and two ells of the respective dimensions of 40×40 and 110×45 feet. There are also various out buildings, utilized for a variety of purposes, the premises being excellently arranged and being equipped throughout with machinery of the most improved type; including a 70 horse engine and three steam boilers, having an aggregate capacity of 200 horse power. Employment is afforded to from 550 to 600 operatives, the output is from 3,000 to 4,000 pairs per day. Messrs. William & J. M. Bent make a leading speciality of the manufacture of fine shoes, and manufacture for Messrs. Potter, White & Bailey, one of the largest houses in the trade. If any curiosity is felt as to the reasons for the enviable reputation held by the productions of this factory it will surely be dispelled by a visit to the premises and a careful investigation of the methods practiced, for nothing is left to chance, but every process is carried out in accordance with a well-arranged system, and from the reception of the raw material to the sending out of the finished article, careful and skillful supervision is constantly provided. The firm manufacture a great variety of styles, and it is evident that the most diverse tastes can be suited from the extensive line they turn out. Beauty, comfort, durability—this is a most desirable combination, and it is not surprising that the productions of this representative concern should be in constantly increasing demand.

Felch Bros., manufacturers of Men's, Boys' and Youth's Wax and Split Brogans and Plow Shoes, Factory and Office, North Main, near Pine Street, Natick, Mass.; Boston Office, 121 Summer Street. —The undertaking carried on by Messrs. Felch Brothers was founded in 1858, and some idea of how the business has developed during the past 32 years may be gained from the fact that the original shop was just 20 feet square, while the present factory contains four floors each of which has an area of about 3,200 square feet. The factory and office are located on North Main street, near Pine, and a most complete plant of the latest improved machinery is utilized, power being furnished by a 40-horse engine and employment being given to 100 assistants, who produce about 1,500 pairs per day. The firm is constituted of Messrs. J. F. Felch, O. A. Felch and Harry Felch, all of whom are natives of Natick. Mr. J. F. Felch was formerly connected with the board of selectmen, and Mr. O. A. Felch is one of the directors of the Natick National Bank, and all the partners are so universally known hereabouts as to render extended personal mention quite unnecessary. They give careful attention to the many details of the business and their products are of uniformly excellent quality; comparing favorably with all others of similar grade in the market. Men's boys' and youths' wax and split brogans and plow shoes are very extensively manufactured, and samples may be seen at No. 121 Summer street, Boston. A well appointed grocery store is maintained by Messrs. Felch Bros., opposite their factory and it is a great public accommodation as the stock is large and varied, the goods excellent and the prices as low as the lowest.

N. R. Gerald, dealer in Stationery, Confectionery, Fancy Goods, Patent Medicines, Cigars and Tobacco, also Agent for Daily and Weekly Papers, Cochituate, Mass.—It is a perfectly safe assertion to make that everybody in Cochituate is entirely familiar with the establishment conducted by Mr. N. R. Gerald, not only because the post office is located on the premises, but also because the assortment of goods offered is so attractive and the prices quoted are so low that the store is very popular among the most discriminating purchasers. Mr. Gerald is a native of Randall, Mass., and has carried on his present business since 1878. In his official capacity as postmaster he is both efficient and accommodating, and spares no pains to make the service as satisfactory as possible, both as regards promptness and accuracy. A large and exceptionally varied stock is carried, comprising stationery, confectionery, fancy goods, patent medicines, cigars and tobacco; and as Mr. Gerald is agent for the daily and weekly papers it will be seen that his store is a decided public accommodation in more respects than one. He quotes the lowest market rates on the various goods he handles, and the latest fashionable novelties in stationery, fancy goods, etc., are always well represented in his stock which, taken as a whole, is one of the most attractive of the kind to be found in this section of the State.

E. A. Atwood, dealer in Groceries, Flour and Grain, Pond Street, Cochituate.—Mr. E. A. Atwood is a native of Natick, and is very widely and favorably known throughout this vicinity, having begun operations in Cochituate in 1878, and holding an enviable reputation as an enterprising business man who employs strictly legitimate methods and makes it an invariable rule to keep faith with his customers at all times. He utilizes premises located on Pond street, and having an area of 1,200 square feet, thus affording ample room for the carrying of a very extensive stock made up of groceries, flour, grain, canned goods, teas, coffees, spices, etc. As Mr. Atwood caters expressly to family trade his goods are selected with unusual care, and being obtained from the most reputable sources can safely be guaranteed to prove strictly as represented in every respect. Table relishes, conserves, sauces, etc., are extensively handled, and the line of canned goods is made up exclusively of the productions of the most reliable packers and includes fruits, vegetables, meats, etc., all of which are warranted to contain no injurious substances of any kind. Choice brands of flour are also largely dealt in; bottom prices being quoted on bag and barrel lots, and grain will be furnished in quantities to suit, all orders being assured prompt and accurate delivery.

J. M. Moore, dealer in Meats and Provisions, also Proprietor of Livery Stable, Cochituate.— The enterprises conducted by Mr. J. M. Moore are among the most useful and popular of all those located in this community, for he gives close personal attention to the supervision of affairs and is consequently enabled to keep the service up to a high standard of efficiency. He is a native of Cochituate, and served in the army during the Rebellion; and in 1884 succeeded Mr. W. C. Neal in the ownership of the meat and provision business which Mr. Moore has since so successfully conducted. The store has an area of about 600 square feet, and always contains a carefully chosen stock, comprising beef, lamb, veal, pork, mutton, hams and fresh and salted meats in general, together with country produce, including all kinds of vegetables in their season. All classes of trade are catered to and the lowest market rates are quoted on the various commodities handled. Mr. Moore also carries on a well-equipped livery stable and is prepared to furnish stylish, comfortable and in every way desirable teams, at short notice and at reasonable rates. He has eight horses available for livery purposes, and employs sufficient assistance to ensure both animals and vehicles being kept in first class condition and to enable him to guarantee prompt and satisfactory service at all times.

H. C. Dean, manufacturer of Brogans and Plow Shoes, Main Street, Cochituate.—The enterprise conducted by Mr. H. C. Dean has been carried on for nearly 30 years and is one of the best known of the various manufacturing undertakings located in this vicinity. It was inaugurated in 1861 by Mr. H. C. Dean, afterwards being continued by Messrs. T. A. & H. C. Dean, who were succeeded by Messrs. C. W. & H. C. Dean, the present proprietor assuming sole control in 1879. He was born in Cochituate, has been a member of the board of selectmen, and for years has been regarded as one of our most truly representative business men. Mr. Dean is engaged in the manufacture of brogans and plow shoes, and utilizes one-half a shop which occupies premises comprising three floors of the dimensions of 20×60 feet. His productions are well known among the trade, and their uniformity of quality makes them popular alike with dealers and consumers for they can safely be guaranteed to prove as represented, and are sure to give entire satisfaction. Mr. Dean is prepared to fill orders at short notice, and to quote the lowest market rates at all times.

C. A. Goodnow, dealer in Boots, Shoes and Rubbers, Furnishings and Dry Goods, Cochituate, Mass.—We are quite sure that the residents of Cochituate will agree with us in considering the establishment conducted by Mr. C. A. Goodnow to be worthy of especially favorable mention, for it is one of the most popular stores in town, and what is still more to the point, its popularity has been attained by the continual practice of strictly legitimate methods. The business was founded a good many years ago, and in 1879 came into the possession of Mr. George A. Leach, who was succeeded by the present proprietor in 1888. Mr. Goodnow was born in Waltham, Mass., and has proved himself to be a careful and discriminating buyer as well as an enterprising dealer since he became identified with his present business, for his stock is always attractive in variety and quality, and his prices are as low as can be quoted on really dependable goods. Among the more prominent articles dealt in may be mentioned boots, shoes and rubbers, furnishings and dry goods, and the very latest fashionable novelties are represented in the assortment offered, together with full lines of staple goods. Competent assistance is employed and prompt and courteous attention is assured to every caller, goods being cheerfully shown at all times. Mr. Goodnow is also agent for W. A. Bird for coal and wood.

R. C. Dean, manufacturer of Brogans and Plow Shoes, Cochituate, Mass.—Among the flourishing and noteworthy concerns devoted to the production of footwear in Cochituate may be mentioned the establishment of R. C. Dean, manufacturer of brogans and plow shoes, and whose products maintain a uniformly high standard of excellence, and as a consequence are in steady and extensive demand throughout the South and West, while the trade affords evidence of constant and substantial increase every year. Mr. Dean, who is a native of Cochituate, is a practical and expert workman, and is thoroughly conversant with every detail of the business. The business was commenced in 1870 by King & Dean, but in 1873 Mr. A. F. Dean assumed full control and thus continued until 1879, when the present proprietor, then only nineteen years of age, became a partner, the two brothers doing business under the firm style of A. F. Dean & Co. In 1882, Mr. R. C. Dean became sole proprietor, the business growing and extending rapidly from the first, until now it is of a most gratifying character. The factory is a three story frame structure, 20×60 feet in dimensions, and is also occupied by Mr. R. C. Dean. Employment is afforded to from 20 to 25 hands. Mr. Dean gives very close personal attention to the business, and the prosperous development of the business is but a just reward.

Cochituate House, J. A. Dupuis, Proprietor, Cochituate, Mass.—It requires no little tact and ability to manage a hotel successfully, for one has all sorts of people to deal with, and what will suit one class of patrons will prove highly obnoxious to another; so it is no wonder that but few men are capable of conducting a really popular house, and that failures are much more frequent than successes. An immediate and pronounced success in this line of business is certainly worthy of more than passing mention, and in this connection we may very fittingly call the attention of our readers to the Cochituate House under its present management, for since Mr. J. A. Dupuis succeeded Mr. William Hardy in the proprietorship of the hotel, in 1889, he has amply proved both his determination and his ability to make the house a popular one in the best sense of the word. Mr. Dupuis is a native of Canada, and evidently has a very clear conception of what the public demand in hotel accommodations, for he has worked hard to improve the service offered at the Cochituate House, and neglects no opportunity to make such changes as careful observation indicates would be desirable. The hotel can accommodate thirty guests, and the facilities now at hand are such that this number of patrons can be satisfactorily catered to at very short notice. The rooms are very comfortably furnished, and the entire premises are kept in neat and attractive condition; while the table is supplied with an abundant variety of substantial food, and the cooking and service are both far superior to the average. The terms of the house are uniformly moderate, and such of our readers as may have occasion to visit Cochituate will best serve their own interests by putting up at this liberally managed hotel.

INDEX TO NOTICES.

www.ingramcontent.com/pod-product-compliance
Lightning Source LLC
Chambersburg PA
CBHW020309090426
42735CB00009B/1276